KEY ASPECTS OF GERMAN BUSINESS LAW

A Manual for Practical Orientation

Edited by
Bernd Tremml and Bernard Buecker

American-German Publishers, LLC

KEY ASPECTS OF GERMAN BUSINESS LAW

A Manual for Practical Orientation

Edited
by

Bernd Tremml, M.C.J.
Attorney at Law
Munich Germany

and Bernard Buecker, Dr. Jur.
Attorney at Law
San Antonio, Texas

1997
American-German Publishers, LLC
Austin, Texas

Published by American-German Publishers, LLC.
P.O.Box 200996
Austin, Texas 78720

List of Authors

DR. MATTHIAS ABRELL

Attorney at Law in Frankfurt am Main, Germany. Senior partner in the law firm Abrell, Wendler, Tremml. His particular area of expertise is German business law and encompasses the full spectrum of legal issues a business enterprise can encounter from the time of its formation until its liquidation.

DR. MICHAEL BIHLER

Attorney at Law in Munich, Germany. He provides legal representation to large international corporations and distribution companies as well as to developers and mid-sized businesses.

BERNARD BUECKER

A Fulbright Scholar at the University of Heidelberg Law School, Mr. Buecker received his law degree from the University of Texas at Austin, and practiced law in Frankfurt, Germany, before opening his office in San Antonio, Texas. He specializes in international litigation particularly in German-American disputes.

DR. ALFRED HAGEN MEYER

Attorney at Law in Munich, Germany. Lecturer on food law at the Ludwig-Maximilian University of Munich and the Technical University of Munich. He serves as advisor and legal counsel to committees and private clients on issues involving food law, industrial property rights and the law of the European Community.

DR. MICHAEL KARGER

Attorney at Law in Munich, Germany. His special areas of expertise include computer law and telecommunications law. Lecturer on the law pertaining to the use of on-line computer services and the Internet.

JOACHIM KNAPP

Attorney at Law in Frankfurt am Main, Germany. He is specialized in the provision of tax advice to German businesses as well as to German subsidiaries of foreign companies and the litigation defense of businesses involved in alleged tax offenses. Examiner for the German Examination Commission for Tax Advisors and consultant to the Hessen Chamber of Tax Advisors.

ANDREAS MEISTERERNST

Attorney at Law in Munich, Germany. His focus is on the drafting of contracts pertaining to the civil, commercial and corporate-law needs of his clientele and in the securing, transfer and recision of governmental permits issued by the Federal Republic of Germany and other European countries.

DR. PAUL MCGUIRE

Ph.D. Purdue Univ., serving as a counsel to the Munich office of the European patent-law firm Meissner, Bolte & Partner.

DR. REINHARD NACKE

Attorney at Law in Düsseldorf, Germany. His special area of expertise lies in the representation of foreign and German companies in all of their legal matters, including particularly questions of internal and European Community law.

DR. BERND TREMML

Attorney at Law, specializing in international law. After graduating from the University of Munich School of Law, he studied at the University of Texas at Austin where he received a Masters of Law degree. As a result of his studies in Texas, Mr. Tremml's foreign clientele primarily include companies from the United States.

MICHAEL WENDLER

Attorney at Law in Düsseldorf, Germany. Senior partner in the law firm Abrell, Wendler, Tremml. His primary focus is on the provision of legal representation to German corporations that operate globally and to foreign companies and associations concerning their business activities in Germany.

General Introduction

This book presents a clear and precise overview of the key aspects of German business law. It was written by attorneys involved in the daily practice of business law in Germany and is aimed at people who wish to orient themselves quickly with the German legal system and the manner in which it impacts business purchases, establishment, operations and liquidations.

The first section of the book is devoted to an explanation of the major issues to be considered in acquiring or establishing a business in Germany, whereas the second section focuses on areas of special consideration. In both sections special attention has been paid to highlighting and explaining the differences between the German legal system and that of the United States, though the intention is to provide information that will prove valuable to all foreigners, particularly business men and women and lawyers advising clients with an interest in doing business in Germany.

Though it is the object of this book to present readers with a general orientation and the foundation for making informed decisions concerning business transactions in Germany, it cannot possibly function as a substitute for case-specific professional advice and by no means purports to do so. Those readers who wish to follow up on any decisions they may have formed on the basis of the material presented here are well advised to seek the guidance of qualified attorneys and tax advisors before entering into any binding obligations.

The Editors

Bernd Tremml
Attorney at Law
Munich, Germany

Ben Buecker
Attorney at Law
San Antonio, Texas

Summary of Contents

PART II

SPECIALIZED LAWS IMPACTING THE FORMATION, ACQUISITION AND OPERATION OF A BUSINESS IN GERMANY

Table of Contents

PART I

HOW TO ESTABLISH OR ACQUIRE A BUSINESS IN GERMANY

PART II

SPECIALIZED LAWS IMPACTING THE FORMATION, ACQUISITION AND OPERATION OF A BUSINESS IN GERMANY

Glossary of German Terms and Abbreviations

A

Abgabenordnung (AO)	Tax Code
Amtsgericht	Court of Small Claims; municipal court
Änderungskündigung	a termination of a contract with the reserved right to renew it under altered conditions
Angestellte	employees; salary earners; "white collar" workers
Aktiengesellschaft (AG)	stock corporation
Aktiengesetz (AktG)	law governing stock issuance
Aktionär	stockholder (of a stock corporation)
Aktie	a share of stock; stock certificate
Arbeiter	laborers; "blue collar" workers
Arbeitserlaubnis	work permit
Arbeitserlaubnisverordnung (AEVO)	Work Permit Regulations
Arbeitsförderungsgesetz (AFG)	Work Promotion Act
Arrest	Freeze Order
Aufenthaltsbefugnis	Authorized residence
Aufenthaltsberechtigung	residence entitlement
Aufenthaltsbewilligung	residence grant
Aufenthaltserlaubnis	residence permit
Aufsichtsrat	supervisory board of a company or corporation
Ausländer	foreigner; alien
Ausländergesetz (AuslG)	Aliens Act
Ausländeramt	Aliens Office
Außenministerium	Department of Foreign Affairs

B

Bergamt	mining authorities
Berufsgenossenschaft	administrative authorities in charge of providing social insurance due to occupational accidents
Betriebsaufgabe	abandonment of a business enterprise
Betriebsrat	works council
Betriebsverfassungsgesetz (BetrVG)	Employee Representation Law
Bezirk	district
BGB-Gesellschaft	see Gesellschaft des bürgerlichen Rechts
Bilanzrichtliniengesetz	Accounting Directives Act
Bundesanstalt für Arbeit	Federal Labor Office
Bundesarbeitsgericht	Federal Labor Court
Bundesministerium für Arbeit und Sozialordnung	Federal Department of Labor and Social Order
Bundesfinanzhof	Federal Finance Court
Bundesgerichtshof	Federal Supreme Court
Bundeskartellamt	Federal Cartel Authority
Bundesrechtsanwaltsgebühre nordnung (BRAGO)	Attorneys' Fee Ordinance
Bürgerliches Gesetzbuch (BGB)	Civil Code
Bundesverfassungsgericht	Federal Constitutional Court

D

Deutsche Angestelltengewerkschaft	White Collar Union
Deutscher Beamtenbund	Civil Servants' Union
Deutsche Bundesbank	Federal Reseve Bank of Germany
Deutscher Gewerkschaftsbund (DGB)	German Association of Industrial Labor Unions

Deutsche Mark (DM)	one German mark (German currency unit)
Duldung	residence toleration
Durchführungsverordnung zum Ausländergesetz (DVAuslG)	Implementation Ordinance of the Aliens Act

E

Einführungsgesetz zum BGB (EGBGB)	Introductory Act to the Civil Code
Einkommenssteuer	personal income tax
Einkommenssteuergesetz	Income Tax Act
Einzelunternehmen	sole proprietorship
Entscheidungen des Bundesgerichtshofs in Zivilsachen (BGHZ)	Decisions of the Federal Court for Civil Cases
Europäisches Patentamt	European Patent Office

F

Finanzamt	tax office; tax authorities

G

Gemeinde	community or municipality
Gerichtsvollzieher	sheriff's officer (official debt collector)
Gesamtbetriebsrat	combined or overall works council (of more than one business unit)
Gesamthandsvermögen	joint ownership (of the property of a partnership)
Gesellschaft des bürgerlichen Rechts (GbR) (also: BGB-Gesellschaft)	civil-law partnership
Gesellschaft mit beschränkter Haftung (GmbH)	limited liability company

Gesellschafter	shareholder (in a limited liability company)
Gesellschafterversammlung	shareholder meeting (limited liability company)
Gesellschaftsvertrag	articles of incorporation
Gesetz	law or act
Gesetz gegen den unlauteren Wettbewerb (UWG)	Unfair Competition Act
Gesetz zur Regelung des Rechts der Allgemeinen Geschäftsbedingungen (AGBG)	Law for the Regulation of Standard Business Terms
Gewerbeaufsichtsamt	Trade Supervision Office
Gewerbeordnung (GewO)	Trade Supervision Law
Gewerbesteuer	business tax
GmbH & Co KG	business organizational form which is a combination of a limited liability company and a limited partnership
GmbH-Gesetz (GmbHG)	GmbH Act (the law governing limited liability companies)
Grundsätze ordnungsgemässer Buchführung	principles of proper accounting
Grundsteuer	real-estate tax

H

Handelsgesetzbuch (HGB)	Commercial Code
Handelsgewerbe	commercial trade enterprise (owned and operated by individuals who are merchants by profession). Governed by the HGB.
Handelsregister	commercial register
Handlungsvollmacht (see also: Prokura)	full power of attorney (to represent an enterprise)

Hauptfürsorgestelle	Head Office for Public Assistance
Hauptversammlung	stockholder meeting (stock corporation)

I

Industriegewerkschaft (IG)	industrial trade union
Industrie- und Handelskammer (IHK)	Chamber of Industry and Commerce
Inhaberaktie	bearer stock certificate
Interessenausgleich	compromise on issues of disagreement involving conflicting interests for example, of employers and employees)

K

Kapitalertragssteuer	capital-yield tax.
Kapitalspiegelmethode	literally: capital-mirroring method. The reflection of the actual net value of a partnership in its fiscal balance (as opposed to using the purchase price as the means of measure).
Kaufmann	merchant
Kommanditgesellschaft (KG)	limited partnership (for merchants)
Kommanditgesellschaft auf Aktien (KGaA)	limited partnership combined with stock
Kommanditist	limited partner (in a Kommanditgesellschaft)
Komplementär	general partner; personally liable partner (in a Kommanditgesellschaft)
Konkurs	bankruptcy
Konkursordnung (KO)	Bankruptcy Act
Kostenordnung (KostO)	Cost Regulation (for notary fees)

Körperschaftssteuer	corporate income tax
Kündigungsschutzgesetz (KSchG)	Termination Protection Act

L

Laienrichter	lay judges
Landgericht	Regional Court
Landkreis	county (approx. equivalent)
Leitende Angestellte	senior executives; managerial employees (with the ability to hire and fire); literally: leading employees
Lohnsteuer	wage tax

M

Mahnverfahren	summary proceeding for debt collection
Markengesetz	Trademark Act
Mehrwertsteuer (MwSt) (also: Umsatzsteuer)	value-added tax (VAT)
Mehrwertsteuergesetz (MwStG)	Value-Added Tax Act
Minderkaufmann	small merchant
Mitbestimmungsgesetz (MitbestG)	Co-Determination Law enabling employee representation in a company's management
Montan-Mitbestimmungsgesetz	Coal-and-Steel Co-Determination Law

N

Namensaktie	registered stock
Notar	notary

O

Offene Handelsgesellschaft (OHG)	general partnership (for merchants)
Oberlandesgericht	Court of Appeals

P

Personengesellschaft	partnership
Prokura	full power of attorney enabling company representation by an employee

R

Rechtsanwalt	attorney at law

S

Sachverständiger	public-appointed experts
Satzung	articles of incorporation of a stock corporation
Schachtelbeteiligung	intercorporate participation; mutual stockholding
Selbstbelieferung	the ability to procure goods oneself
Solidaritätszuschlag	solidarity contribution
Stammaktie	common stock
Stammkapital	nominal capital of a business enterprise
Steuer	tax
Steuerberater	tax advisor
Stille Gesellschaft	silent or dormant partnership
Stuttgarter Verfahren	Stuttgart Procedure (a way of assessing the value of a business, which was once the standard procedure in Germany but has recently fallen out of use due to its inaccuracy pitfalls)

U

Umsatzsteuer	value-added tax (VAT). Literally: sales tax.
Umwandlung	transformation of a business enterprise from one organizational form to another
Urhebergesetz (UrhG)	Copyright Act

V

vereidigter Buchprüfer	certified bookkeeper
Verfassung	Constitution
Vermögensübertragung	transfer of corporate assets and liabilities into public ownership
Verschmelzung	corporate merger
Verschmelzung durch Aufnahme	take over; a merger with at least one other company
Verschmelzung durch Neubildung	consolidation of one corporation with another for the purpose of forming an entirely new corporation
Vorschuß	retainer
Vorstand	board of management
Vorzugsaktien	preferred stock

W/X/Y/Z

Wirtschaftsprüfer	certified public accountant (CPA)
Zweigniederlassung	branch office

Preface

THE INVESTMENT CLIMATE IN THE FEDERAL REPUBLIC OF GERMANY

by
Friedrich W. Kuhlmann

German American Chamber of Commerce of the Southern United States, Inc. [1]

The Federal Republic of Germany is reported as Europe's largest producer and customer as well as its main economic link to the newly emerging eastern markets. The latter is certainly a merit of the large investments made in the eastern part of the country, both by governmental and private economic entities.

Since July of 1990, the German Federal Government has transferred more than two hundred billion dollars to the former GDR. Continuous ongoing support is currently planned in the form of one hundred billion dollars per annum for the forthcoming years. That financial aid will flow primarily into high-rise and underground construction and reconstruction, road development, environmental rescue work and the modernization and expansion of the existing but as yet still comparatively antiquated and undeveloped telecommunications infrastructure. Through these efforts, the eastern German states will possibly meet the contemporary western standards within just a few years.

---

[1] German American Chamber of Commerce of the Southern United States, 5599 San Felipe, Suite 510, Houston, TX 77056 USA

And, even though these investments are making up for considerable burdens on the taxpayers and the German economy, the country as a whole is still retaining its number-one-position among its European economic competitors. So, it can be stated that reunification is pushing the country forward economically.

Another strong influence on the German economy was the opening of the "Free European Domestic Market" on January 1, 1993 in accordance with the Maastrich Treaty. Since then, the fifteen Member States of the European Community form a unitary market without national duties and trade barriers. In accordance with the Treaty of Rome, the free movement of capital and labor within the Community are now ensured as is the harmonization of the Member States' economic policies, legal, taxation and social-welfare systems.

In recent years, the European Community has been increasingly active in its efforts to harmonize, unify and standardize the corporate and business laws of its Member States. One of the most notable achievements in this arena has been the successful establishment of standardized minimum requirements for corporate financial reports. In addition, guidelines known as "directives" have been adopted in the areas of consumer protection, fair trade practices, antitrust regulation and taxation, which every one of the Member States has agreed to legislatively incorporate nationally.

The free-market economic system forms the basis of both the German and the overall European Community economy. And that implies, of course, that State intervention in private business affairs is minimized to the highest possible extent. It also implies free trade on a global basis — virtually anyone the world over can invest in

Germany or get started in business in the country if they so wish. Germany not only welcomes the establishment of foreign-owned businesses but guarantees the owners of them that they and their enterprises will be treated no differently than if they were national. It grants them identical rights and commits them to equal obligations. Lenient German trade laws allow foreign corporations to purchase and own the total capital stock of a German corporation, company or even small business endeavors. Financial transactions are furthermore completely free of federally imposed restrictions. Germany's currency-flow gates are wide open and without border controls or limitations of any kind. These factors in combination with the country's fundamentally rock-solid economy, central position within Europe, strong economic and political commitment and ties to the rest of Western Europe and the United States make Germany what it is today — a key world market and a country in which mid- and long-term foreign investments generally tend to reap rewarding returns. As a strategically positioned gateway to the East of Europe, it offers additional advantages, opportunities and perspectives to pioneering entrepreneurs and expansion-oriented corporations. Despite the worldwide recession and current inflationary pressure, Germany's economic, political and social-welfare systems remain stable by global comparison. The standard and quality of life in Germany continue to remain high, statistically and objectively, despite the economic hardships it has incurred and is still incurring through its reunification process. The overall stability of the country, its highly skilled work force, great universities, strategic location and economic leadership combined with its support of free trade are just a few of the obvious reasons why many foreign companies have chosen and continue to chose Germany as a home base for their European subsidiary locations. International comparisons based on objective, bottom-line results clearly show that Germany, despite its comparatively higher labor costs and shorter working hours, is a very attractive place to start an enterprise, locate a European subsidiary, buy an existing local business or invest in a corporation.

This book will be of great assistance to those interested in doing business in the European Union, and is practical resource for knowledge of German law as well.

Introduction

OVERVIEW OF THE GERMAN LEGAL SYSTEM AND ITS ROLE IN LIGHT OF GERMANY'S MEMBERSHIP IN THE EUROPEAN COMMUNITY

Foreign business people who are interested in starting a business or otherwise investing in Germany might be attracted by the prospect of expanding into other European markets from there, which is made possible by Germany's membership in the EC, yet they might be concerned at the same time about the implications of the dual European and German legal systems. They might ask themselves, for instance, whether a German venture requires familiarization with two, often conflicting bodies of law and walking a tightrope between them or if businesses in Germany frequently have to deal with administrative authorities at both the national and international levels with regard to the same transaction. The answer to such questions is „no." Given the structure of the European Community (EC) and particularly the manner in which EC institutions pass laws, an investment in Germany does not involve investors in a legal quagmire.

As a fundamental principal, the European Community and its institutions possess the power to pass legislation concerning only those areas in which an express delegation of national authority exists. For this reason alone, large numbers of regulatory areas remain outside of EC control. For example, most civil, criminal and administrative laws remain the sole province of the Member States. In general,

EC authority is limited to those regulatory areas which are essential to the establishment of a common market. Furthermore, the laws the EC has passed have tended to take the form of directives. As will be explained in detail in Chapter 10, directives do not, as a general principal, take effect until after they have been incorporated into national law. This special characteristic of directives is intended to give the Member States the flexibility of choosing the manner in which the objectives of a directive become law in their own country, the manner that is most compatible with their particular legal system. For individuals and business enterprises alike, it is often not easy to recognize if a national law is based on a European directive or not. In sum, EC directives do *not* constitute an overlay of regulations, which investors must familiarize themselves with separately, but rather comprise an integral part of a Member State's national law.

Much the same applies to those areas in which the EC has enacted a type of legislation known as a "regulation." A regulation does not require incorporation into national law in order to be effective, yet is, as a rule, implemented by the national authorities. For example, if a German administrative authority applies an EC regulation in its dealings with German residents and they feel an error has been made, they can take action only against the national authority and, in doing so, usually operate solely within the German administrative or judicial systems.

For these reasons, the direct effect of European Community law on German residents or businesses is relatively small. That is not to say, however, that the EC's influence should be downplayed. The numerous areas of law impacting the establishment and operation of businesses in Germany, which are the subject matter of this book, are often reflective of EC law. Nevertheless, for the most part, EC laws have been incorporated into national law and are subject to Germany's legal system. And it is within this system that foreign investors will predominantly conduct their business transactions.

For the most part, Germany's legal system is stable and smooth working. In contrast to the U.S. legal system, which is based on Anglo-Saxon law, or common law, the basis for Germany's legal system is the Continental European legal tradition. The primary difference between the two systems is that the Continental European legal system has historically been characterized as one based on the codification of laws as opposed to case law. In accordance with the Continental tradition, the German legal system consists essentially of written laws. Nearly all potential regulatory areas are the subject of formal and detailed codification. Many of Germany's legal codes are the final product of literally decades upon decades of careful deliberation and refinement. This offers foreign entrepreneurs and investors considerable advantages. German law is so clearly structured and transparent that contract terms can be standardized to a very large extent. And, since all the standard practices and regulations governing the conduction of business are codified in the German Civil Code (BGB, or "Bürgerliches Gesetzbuch"), if no special terms are agreed upon between the parties, the terms and provisions of the BGB automatically apply. In other words, whereas in the U.S., business contracts require the clear and detailed statement of all the terms the parties agree to, contracts in Germany tend to be considerably shorter, which lowers their drafting costs accordingly.

As in the U.S., it is the task of the courts to interpret the written law. Because a number of German codes are more than a hundred years old, the case law pertaining to certain individual provisions of them is very extensive. Whereas the courts have the primary task of interpreting the statutes, regulations and Constitution, they also play a role in filling in the gaps of laws where necessary. As a rule, however, the reliance on precedents, or case law, plays a much smaller role in the German legal system than in American jurisprudence, since German laws are so explicitly detailed and codified.

The sharp differentiation between the various areas of law in Germany and the separate codification of them have led to a strict division of subject-matter jurisdiction among the different types of courts. As in the U.S., there are separate civil courts responsible for deciding legal disputes amongst private persons, and there are criminal courts for ruling on criminal prosecutions brought by the State against individuals. In contrast to the U.S. legal system, however, there are also separate court systems for administrative matters or legal disputes involving measures taken by public authorities against residents, for labor-law and financial matters. Germany has a special body of law governing taxation and a court system specialized in trying tax cases as well. It should also be noted that, in contrast to the U.S. judicial system, there is no duality between state and federal courts. In Germany, their areas of jurisdiction are clearly kept separate. Each of the various court systems has its own supreme court. The Constitutional Court is the final authority above each of them.

The judges who serve on the courts are judges by profession and are specialized in one type of law. They do not rotate from one type of court to another, as U.S. judges do, but generally serve on only one type of court throughout their careers. They are not elected but rather appointed by the government of the particular state of Germany where the court is located. Germany does not make use of the jury process. In certain cases, however, the judges are assisted in making their decisions by common citizens who do not necessarily have a legal background of any kind ("Laienrichter") and who are chosen to serve on the court for a limited time period.

Regardless of which type of court is handling a particular dispute, the parties' trial preparation consists primarily in the drafting and presentation of legal briefs in which evidence is presented and the issues in dispute are argued. In so doing, the parties rely on the court's special procedural rules. Each type of court has its own rules determining its case procedure, the kind of evidence it will admit, etc. The courts make extensive use of independent public-appointed experts („Sachverständiger"), whose professional input almost always influences the ruling to a very large extent and often determines the outcome of a case. Due in part to the judicial system's reliance on the parties' briefs, the reports of independent experts and other written submissions, the trial itself (in particular the in-court presentation of live testimony and other evidence) takes considerably less time and involves less costs than U.S. court proceedings. This will be discussed extensively in Chapter 14. With the exception of criminal cases, most trials last no longer than one or two days.

An overview of Germany's legal system would not be complete without a few comments about the governmental administrative apparatus. The Federal Republic of Germany is, as its name expresses, a federal state. That means that legislative powers are divided between the federal government and each of the country's sixteen states. The most important areas of law are the exclusive domain of the federal government. However, because the individual states of Germany are generally vested with the authority to enforce federal laws, and the majority of the administrative offices necessary to accomplish this task are established by the states, the states have an important influence on the interpretation and development of federal laws. Similar to the state subdivisions in the U.S., the states of Germany are comprised of districts ("Bezirke"), counties ("Landkreise") and communities ("Gemeinde"), whereby a striking difference between the two administrative systems is in many cases the higher degree of authority and competence exercised by the more local and regional units in Germany, which often allows them to take action and make decisions affecting both residents and businesses more efficiently and quickly.

In conclusion, it can be said that the legal system in Germany is precisely structured. Its areas of court jurisdiction are clearly defined and its laws so explicitly codified that overlapping and ambiguities are largely ruled out. That makes it relatively easy for foreigners to orient themselves within the system, and they will find the drafting of business contracts to be a relatively swift and inexpensive process, especially when compared with the situation in the U.S., where effort and costs generally tend to be considerably higher, not least of all because its laws allow a vastly wider degree of interpretation and because all the terms of agreement must be contained in the contract itself. In Germany, however, the terms of the Civil Code (BGB) regulating contracts automatically come into effect in the absence of other terms. Contracts between business partners are necessary only if and insofar as the parties wish to agree to terms that differ from the standard provisions of the BGB. As pertains to business operations, the clearly structured German system encourages fair, free trade and the minimization of conflicts.

PART I.

HOW TO ESTABLISH OR ACQUIRE A BUSINESS IN GERMANY

Chapter 1

RECOGNIZED FORMS OF BUSINESS ORGANIZATIONS

Bernd Tremml and Bernard Buecker

I. Overview of Business Forms Available

The Federal Republic of Germany recognizes a variety of business organizational forms. Each of them has its own particular justification for existence based on specific economic considerations. It is therefore important for foreign business people who intend to establish a company in Germany to evaluate the various business forms available – for instance, in terms of their organizational structure, liability and methods of taxation – and determine which of them is most suitable for the enterprise they have in mind.

German law basically differentiates between business organizational forms which have the characteristic of a partnership ("Personengesellschaft" is the general term for partnership) and those which have the characteristics of a corporation. In contrast to the partnership forms, the corporate ones each possess the status of a separate legal entity. Another major distinction is that, as a general rule, the shareholders of businesses organized as corporations possess limited liability equal to the amount of capital they have invested in the business, whereas a partnership's creditors can lay claim to the personal assets of each of the partners if necessary.

The corporate forms are:

- the GmbH, which is an abbreviation for "Gesellschaft mit beschränkter Haftung" and means "limited liability company,"
- the AG, which is an abbreviation for "Aktiengesellschaft" and means "stock corporation."

The partnership forms are:

- the GbR, which is an abbreviation for "Gesellschaft des bürgerlichen Rechts" and possesses characteristics of a joint venture,
- the OHG, which is an abbreviation for „Offene Handelsgesellschaft" and possesses characteristics of a general partnership,
- the KG, which is an abbreviation for "Kommanditgesellschaft" and possesses characteristics of a limited partnership,"
- the "Einzelunternehmen," or "sole proprietorship,"
- the "Stille Gesellschaft," or "silent partnership."

Germany furthermore recognizes two types of business organizational forms which are a mixture of the corporate and partnership forms:

- the GmbH & Co. KG

  - and -

- the KGaA, which is an abbreviation for "Kommanditgesellschaft auf Aktien" and is a type of limited partnership combined with stock.

The most common business form used in Germany today is the GmbH (limited liability company), which is due to the facts that a GmbH is relatively easy to establish and operate and is an appropriate organizational form for almost all types of business. There are a comparatively smaller number of stock corporations in Germany since that form is more suitable for very large enterprises such as banks and insurance companies. The partnership forms are less often found among larger enterprises because the owners of them or participants in them wish to avoid being personally and fully liable for all of the debts of the business.

II. Corporate Forms of Business Organizations

A. Limited liability company ["Gesellschaft mit beschränkter Haftung" (GmbH)]

1. Nature

The legal basis for the limited liability company (GmbH) is contained in the GmbH Act (GmbHG), first adopted in 1898 and substantially revised in 1980. As an incorporated business entity, the GmbH itself possesses rights and obligations and is liable for all of its debts to the full extent of its corporate assets. It also may pursue and defend legal actions in its own name (Par. 13 GmbHG).

In the GmbH's articles of incorporation ("Gesellschaftssvertrag"), the shareholders set the amount of nominal capital which is to be paid into the corporation by each of them. The individual shareholders are then liable for the company's obligations only in the amount of their committed capital investment. The GmbH cannot enforce an obligation against any shareholder in excess of that amount. Under German law, the shares of a GmbH cannot be quoted on stock exchanges.

The articles of incorporation can make special regulations for the individual needs and requirements of the company and its owners to the extent they do not conflict with the provisions of the GmbH Act.

2. Regular formation procedure

A GmbH can be established for any lawful purpose by one or more people. Its founder(s), or initial shareholders, may be natural persons or legal entities, residents or non-residents, German or foreign citizens. The law does not limit the number of shareholders who may participate in a GmbH.

The structure and operations of a GmbH are governed by its articles of incorporation. The first step in the process of forming a GmbH is the drafting of its articles by its founders (shareholders). The articles must be signed by each of the shareholders and approved by a notary. In addition to a statement of the name, location and purpose of the company, the articles must state the total amount of the nominal capital („Stammkapital") and the percent or share of it that each shareholder has agreed to pay in return for shares in the business. The name chosen for the company must directly relate to the company's purpose or contain the names of at least one of the shareholders. It is further required that the company name contain the designation "GmbH" ["company with limited liability." (See Par. 4 GmbHG.)].

The company comes into actual existence and is able to reap the benefits of having its liabilities limited to its assets only after it has been registered in the commercial register ("Handelsregister") located in the district court of the company's place of business. Before that time, the founding partners are personally liable for their own business transactions during the GmbH's "formation stage" (Par. 11 GmbHG).

Entry into the commercial register requires the submission of a formal application by the managing director(s) with all the necessary attachments, including:

- the articles of incorporation,
- original documents expressing the authority of any person to act on behalf of the founding shareholders (power of attorney) or a certified copy of the same,
- a confirmation of the appointment of the managing director(s) if the appointment(s) are not stated in the articles of incorporation,
- specimen signatures of the managing director(s),
- a statement as to whether the managing director(s) are personally empowered to represent the company or whether they can do so only in conjunction with others,
- a list of the shareholders, including their full name, profession and address as well as the share amount of the nominal capital investment guaranteed by each of them,
- the assurance that the combined amount of cash and non-cash assets required by law before the GmbH can be legally registered has indeed been paid into the company and is available for use by its management. (The law requires that at least 25% of each share and 50% of the nominal capital has been paid-in before the company can be registered unless non-cash investments have been arranged and agreed upon).
- In the case of a one-person GmbH the cash and non-cash contained in the company must equal DM 50,000.— [fifty thousand German marks] at the time of registration.
- Assurance that the total amount of investment shares (the nominal capital of the business, or „Stammkapital") equals at least DM 50,000.
- A special non-cash investment report verifying the actual value of any non-cash investments.

If all of the above requirements are met, the GmbH will be registered and the registration automatically announced in a nation-wide publication.

3. Capital Structure

a) Share capital

The 1980 reform of the GmbH Act raised the statutory minimum amount of capital that must be invested by the owners in return for shares to DM 50,000.— and the minimum that each single shareholder must invest to DM 500.

The capital may be paid in cash, in kind (non-cash) or in a combination of the two. When a non-cash investment has been agreed to, a special report has to be presented so that the actual worth of the non-cash capital investments can be evaluated by the registry court.

It is not required that the nominal capital (upwards of DM 50,000.—) be divided into equal amounts. Each share can be ascribed a value equal to the investment the individual shareholder has agreed to make and stated accordingly in the articles of incorporation. Shares can be subsequently split into units of less value and transferred to others, however, only with the approval of the company (Par. 17 GmbHG).

b) Transfer of shares

The shares of a GmbH are freely transferable and inheritable (Par. 15 GmbHG). However, the articles of incorporation can stipulate that the transfer is conditional upon the consent of the GmbH or the other shareholders. A change of shareholders does not affect the continuing existence of the company. The company can acquire its own shares only if the share capital is fully paid-up, sufficient funds beyond the stated share capital exist, and the statutory reserves for its own shares can be maintained. In order to be valid, the transfer of a share (in whole or in part) must be executed before a notary.

c) Increase and reduction of nominal capital

The shareholders can increase or reduce the nominal capital figure as cited in the articles of incorporation, however, only in so far as they do not reduce it below the legally required minimum of DM 50,000. The decision to raise or lower the capital value of a company requires a vote of three-fourths of the shareholder votes cast unless the articles of incorporation provide otherwise. The amendment to the articles of incorporation must be filed with the court so that the corresponding changes can be made in the commercial register (Par. 54 GmbHG).

In the event that the nominal capital amount is to be increased, each of the shareholders must present a notarized statement that they are willing to raise their personal investments proportionate to the overall increase and according to the new value of their shares (Par. 55 GmbHG). Moreover, new shareholders may be added to the GmbH at the time of an increase in the GmbH's nominal capital value.

In order for a reduction in the nominal amount of share capital to take effect, the shareholder resolution authorizing it must be announced in the public journals officially responsible for publishing commercial-register matters. Any creditors who oppose the reduction are entitled to have their outstanding claims satisfied. The law proscribes that one year must have elapsed after the final public announcement before the GmbH can file an application to have the decreased capital amount officially noted in the commercial register (Par. 58 GmbHG).

4. Representation and management

Representation and management of a GmbH result from the cooperation of the following official corporate bodies: managing director(s), shareholders and supervisory board.

a) Managing director ("Geschäftsführer")

Because the managing director is the only person entitled to represent the company in and out of court (Par. 35 GmbHG), the GmbH must -- either in the articles of incorporation or by separate resolution -- appoint one or more managing director(s) in order for the company to be able to act. The managing director must be a natural person with unlimited capacity to enter into legal transactions (Par. 6 GmbHG) and may but need not be a shareholder of the company.

German corporate law differentiates between the external authority of the managing director and his or her internal rights and obligations. This means that, although the authority of the managing director may be and often is restricted by the provisions of the articles of incorporation, shareholder resolutions or the managing director's employment contract, such restrictions are of no effect concerning the managing director's interactions with third parties.

The managing director of a GmbH has the legal obligation to perform his or her duties with the "diligence of a prudent businessperson." And even though the business transactions of the managing director(s) are valid with respect to third parties, if the directors violate their obligations to perform their duties carefully, they are jointly and severally liable to the company for any resulting damage. Under the general provisions of German tort law, the managing director's personal liability for wrongful acts committed against third persons is limited to situations in which he or she has personally acted.

The other situations in which the managing director can be held personally liable to third parties are:

1) if in the registration of a newly formed company the managing director has officially stated that one-fourth (or more) of the share capital has been paid by the shareholders and this is not the case (Par. 64 GmbHG) or
2) the managing director fails to declare bankruptcy within three weeks after he or she has learned or could have learned that the company is either unable to pay its debts and/or that its liabilities exceed its assets.

If the managing director has been appointed by a shareholder resolution, the appointment can be withdrawn by a new resolution. If the managing director has been appointed in the articles of incorporation, then, based on the rule that every change of the articles requires a 75% majority vote, he or she can be removed only by a three-quarters vote of the voting shareholders. Entry into the commercial register is necessary for all changes affecting the identity or representation authority of the managing director(s) (Par. 39 GmbHG).

b) Shareholders ("Gesellschafter")

The rights of the shareholders within the corporation, particularly with respect to the management of the business, derive from the articles of incorporation in so far as they are consistent with statutory provisions (Par. 45 GmbHG). All shareholder resolutions must be adopted in a general meeting. Unless otherwise provided in the articles of incorporation, the managing director calls the shareholder meetings by sending registered letters to the shareholders at least one week in advance of the meeting. In their meetings, the shareholders are entitled to reach decisions which concern and impact the day-to-day operations of the business and to exercise complete discretion in issuing management instructions. There are particular issues which can be resolved only in a shareholder meeting. They include the appointment and dismissal of management, the granting and cancellation of "Prokuras" (full powers of attorney as defined in Par. 48 HGB, the Commercial Code), the institution of claims for damages against the managing director or shareholders, the approval of financial statements and the agreement to the manner in which any dividends are to be distributed.

In order to be effective, shareholder decisions require a majority approval of those shareholders who participated in the vote (Par. 47 GmbHG). Proxy voting is allowed. If all company shares are controlled by one shareholder, that shareholder must prepare and sign minutes without undue delay following the passage of a resolution.

Shareholders have the right, upon request, to be informed of business affairs by the company's management and to inspect the company books and records (Par. 51 a GmbHG). If management believes, however, that providing specific information could substantially impair business operations or otherwise be detrimental to the company, it can refuse the request. Any shareholder who has not been given the requested information or permission to inspect the books is entitled to file a court action seeking judicial resolution of the conflict.

c) Supervisory board ("Aufsichtsrat")

German law does not always require that a GmbH have a supervisory board. Any decision to establish such a board, however, must be reflected in the articles of incorporation. A GmbH must have a supervisory board if it is a capital-investment company. There are also cases in which the "Co-Determination Law" ("Mitbestimmungsgesetz") makes such a board mandatory. This law, which requires that certain companies allow employee participation in management, will be described in more detail later. One variation of it, for instance, is The Coal-and-Steel Co-Determination Law ("Montan-Mitbestimmungsgesetz"), which applies to GmbHs that are engaged in coal or steel production. The supervisory board must consist of an equal number of shareholder and labor representatives and a neutral person. The neutral person may but need not be the chairman of the board.

Under the German Co-Determination Law, GmbHs with more than 2,000 employees must have a supervisory board consisting of an equal number of shareholder and labor representatives.

The Business Unit Constitution Law ("Betriebsverfassungsgesetz") requires that GmbHs with more than five hundred employees install a supervisory board comprised of a two-third majority of shareholder-elected members and a one-third minority of employee-elected members.

Whether a supervisory board has been created at the discretion of the shareholders or is required by law, its primary role is to represent the GmbH when dealing with the managing director(s).

5. Accounting and auditing

The managing director is responsible for ensuring that the GmbH has proper account books and balance sheets. Accounting and auditing laws pertaining to GmbHs are contained in the Commercial Code (HGB), the GmbH Act (GmbHG) and the tax laws as modified in 1986 by the Accounting Directives Act ("Bilanzrichtliniengesetz").

In accordance with sound accounting principles, the company must keep proper account books showing all transactions, assets and liabilities. At the date of the GmbH's formation and at the end of each financial year, an inventory and a balance sheet must be prepared. These financial records must be kept for ten years; commercial correspondence and invoices must be kept for six years.

In terms of the exact type of accounting requirements, German law differentiates between small, medium and large companies. Which of these size categories a company falls into depends on its profit, sales and number of employees. If the company is a so-called "large company," its accounts must be audited by a certified public accountant („Wirtschaftsprüfer"), and its annual financial statement, its management report as well as the proposals and decisions on the distribution of profits must be made public according to the Accounting Directives Act. Mid-sized companies, on the other hand, may obtain the services of a certified bookkeeper („vereidigter Buchprüfer"). There are no laws requiring audits in small companies.

6. Liquidation

a) Reasons for dissolution

A GmbH can be dissolved at any time by a resolution passed by three-fourths of the shareholders participating in the vote unless otherwise stipulated in the articles of incorporation. Furthermore, upon the application of shareholders holding at least 10 % of the share capital, the company can be dissolved by court order. The issuance of such an order requires that the court finds either that it has become impossible for the GmbH to accomplish its purpose or that other substantial reasons stemming from the prevailing conditions in the company exist which are substantial enough to justify its dissolution.

Bankruptcy proceedings are another cause of the dissolution of a GmbH. If, however, the bankruptcy proceedings are terminated after the conclusion of a compulsory settlement or upon motion of a debtor, then the shareholders may elect not to dissolve the company.

b) Insolvency and liquidation

When a GmbH becomes insolvent and the managing director has filed a declaration of bankruptcy, the court appoints liquidators. When a GmbH is dissolved for a reason other than the initiation of bankruptcy proceedings, the managing director automatically assumes the role of liquidator. During the process of liquidation, the company must be clearly identified and recognizable as being in a state of liquidation.

The liquidator's duties are to terminate current business, discharge all obligations of the dissolved company, collect its accounts receivable and convert all assets into cash. It is also his or her duty to prepare a balance sheet at the beginning of the liquidation process, once every year thereafter and at the conclusion of the process.

Except in the case of bankruptcy proceedings, the dissolution of the company must be registered in the commercial register, and a notice requesting creditors to file any claims must be published three times. The GmbH's assets may not be distributed to the shareholders until the expiration of one year following the third publication. At this time (and assuming the liquidation process has otherwise reached the point where the assets can be distributed), all remaining assets are to be distributed among the shareholders in proportion to their share interests.

As mentioned above, all the books and records of a company must be retained for ten years. Following a liquidation process, those documents are to be delivered to a former shareholder or third party for safe-keeping.

7. Conclusion

The limited liability company with its simple formation procedure and structure is the most suitable legal form for foreign businesses wanting to limit the risks of their activities to the amount of capital they are willing to invest in the Federal Republic of Germany.

B. Stock corporations [“Aktiengesellschaft” (AG)]

1. Nature

The formation and constitution of an AG are governed by legislation entitled the “Aktiengesetz” (AktG). Similar to the GmbH, an AG is an incorporated business entity with its own legal personality. Only its corporate assets are available to satisfy the liability of the company to its creditors. The stockholders (“Aktionäre”) bear no personal liability.

The nominal capital („Grundkapital”) of an AG is divided into stocks (“Aktien”) which, unlike the shares of a GmbH, may but need not be quoted on the stock exchange. The stocks are freely transferable, which makes the occupations and backgrounds of the individual stockholders completely irrelevant.

The stock corporation is the best business organizational form in Germany for large enterprises. It offers the best legal basis for an international business.

2. Formation and registration

An AG can be formed by one or more persons who are willing to subscribe for stock in return for their capital investment. These persons may be individuals or corporate entities, residents of Germany or non-residents.

At the beginning of the formation procedure, the founders have to draft articles of incorporation ("Satzung") which primarily must include : the AG's name, location, business objective and amount of stock capital (face amount as well as the number of stock certificates issued and their initial subscription price). The company's name usually reflects its activities and must be followed by the acronym "AG." In most cases, the designated seat of the corporation must be the place where the company intends to maintain an establishment, where its management is to be located or from where the administration of the company will be conducted.

The articles of incorporation must have been recorded by a German notary before the corporation can be officially formed and registered. The founders appoint the first supervisory board ("Aufsichtsrat"), which is then empowered to appoint the initial board of management ("Vorstand"). In addition to these two organs, the stockholders themselves, who are empowered to take action in general meetings known as "Hauptversammlungen," comprise the third organ of an AG. The members of the supervisory board and initial board of management are charged with examining the act of formation and rendering a written formation report. The formation must also be examined by one or more court-appointed formation auditors if one of the following circumstances exist:

- a member of the board of management or the supervisory board is also one of the founders of the corporation,
- a member of the board of management or supervisory board had stock earmarked for him- or herself, either directly or indirectly, during the formation stage,
- a member of the board of management or the supervisory board will receive a special advantage
- or the formation involves non-cash investments or related non-cash acquisitions.

The AG must apply for registration in the commercial register ("Handelsregister") of the local court responsible for the district in which the company is located. The application must be signed by all the founders as well as by each member of the board of management and the supervisory board. All underlying documents, including the articles of incorporation, must accompany the application for registration.

The registration will be granted only if the required percentage of the initial stock subscription has been duly paid-in. That amounts to at least 25% of the par value of the stocks in the case of cash subscriptions and 100% in the case of non-cash investments.

The AG comes into existence as a legal entity upon entry in the commercial register (Par. 41 AktG). Until that time, anyone who acts on behalf of the corporation is personally liable.

3. Capital structure

a) Stock capital

The statutory minimum capital amount, which must be paid-in at the time of registration, is one hundred thousand German Marks (DM 100,000.--). The capital is divided into par value shares, which can have a nominal value of DM 50, DM 100 or any sum divisible by DM 100. The face value of the shares and their total amount must be expressed in German Marks.

Membership in an AG is documented by stock certificates. Both common stock ("Stammaktien") and preferred stock ("Vorzugsaktien") may be issued either as bearer stock certificates ("Inhaberaktien") or as registered stock certificates ("Namensaktien"). In general, one share of stock entitles its owner to one vote on issues addressed in the stockholder meeting ("Hauptversammlung"). Preferred stock, however, may be stipulated as non-voting stock. Bearer stock is the most common type of stock issued by German stock corporations. The shares cannot be issued before they have been registered and the purchaser has paid-in the full issue price.

b) Transfer of stockholdings

Bearer stock can be freely transferred, and any attempt to limit that transferability is strictly prohibited. The transfer of registered stock, however, can be limited with the consent of the company, provided its articles of incorporation explicitly allow for such regulation in order to guarantee that the company maintains control and influence over its members and thus over its own operations.

In practice, bearer stock is usually offered by banks and the original certificates left deposited with them. The banks then collect the dividends on behalf of the investors. Stockholders who own a relatively small number of a corporation's total shares generally tend to give proxies to their banks to exercise their voting rights. Such proxies are valid for a maximum of fifteen months at a time and can be withdrawn at any time within that period (Par. 135 AktG).

c) Increase and decrease of nominal capital

An increase or decrease in the nominal capital amount requires a resolution passed by a three-fourth majority of the votes cast at a stockholder meeting. An application for an increase or decrease must be filed with the commercial register. The new nominal capital amount becomes effective at the moment of registration.

The easiest way to increase the share capital is by issuing new shares against contributions, which may be in cash or non-cash. In the case of non-cash investments, the property, the name of the person from whom the AG acquires it and the nominal amount of the stock shares granted in return for it must be noted in the shareholder resolution to increase the company's nominal capital value on (Par. 183 AktG).

Other ways to acquire new capital are through the issuance of convertible bonds, profit-sharing bonds or profit participating certificates.

4. Representation and management

a) Board of management ("Vorstand")

The board of management consists of one or more persons. The management board of a AG with a stock capital of more than three million German Marks generally must consist of at least two persons. In order to maintain the independence of both of the boards, a member of the board of management cannot serve as a member of the supervisory board and vice versa. The members of the board of management are usually appointed by the supervisory board for a period of five years.

The board of management is responsible for managing the business, handling all general administrative matters and representing the corporation in its dealing with third parties as well as in all judicial actions. The power of its authority may not be limited in its dealings with third parties. It is possible, however, to provide in the article of incorporation that certain actions require the approval of another organ of the AG.

The members of the board of management are each required to act with the diligence and care of a prudent and conscientious manager. Transactions entered into in violation of this standard of care, while valid and binding on the AG, make the members of the board of management personally liable to the corporation for any damage it has sustained as a result of their careless behavior. Board members cannot be held responsible for having breached their standard of care, however, if they have acted on a valid resolution of the stockholders.

b) Supervisory board ("Aufsichtsrat")

In contrast to the law governing GmbHs (GmbHG), the law pertaining to AGs (AktG) requires that every AG establish a supervisory board. This board's primary functions are the appointment and dismissal of board of management ("Vorstand"), supervision of executive management, approval of the financial statements prepared by the executive managers and approval of any special transactions enumerated in the articles of incorporation.

The size of the supervisory board may vary between three and twenty-one members, depending on the size of the corporation. In AGs which employ less than 2,000 persons, the size of the board depends on the nominal value, or share capital, of the company. If the value of share capital is three million German Marks or less, the law requires a board consisting of three but no more than nine members. If the capital value lies between three and twenty million German Marks, the law requires that between nine and fifteen members be appointed. Corporations with a capital value of more than twenty millions German Marks are required to appoint between fifteen and twenty-one members.

German law gives employees of larger corporations the right to vote for a portion of the supervisory board and/or to serve on it through representation. The membership of employees on the supervisory board is generally dependent on the overall number of people employed by the corporation. Certain industries have special regulations governing employee participation.

c) Stockholder meeting ("Hauptversammlung")

The general meeting of the stockholders must be held annually and within eight months after the end of the business year. The meeting must take place in Germany and generally at the place where the AG has its registered office. In addition to the general meeting, extraordinary stockholder meetings can be called by the supervisory board or by stockholders holding at least five per cent of the common stock.

The stockholders, acting in concert at their general meeting, are responsible for the appointment and removal of their supervisory board representatives, the election of auditors, the formal approval of actions taken by the supervisory board and the board of management during the preceding business year and decisions concerning the distribution of profits. The most important of the statutory powers that are the exclusive rights of the stockholders are the rights to

- amend the articles of incorporation,
- reduce or increase the stock capital,
- liquidate the AG.

5. Accounting and auditing

Legal requirements imposed on an AG's accounting system are primarily found in the Commercial Code (HGB, part two), the AktG and the tax laws. The second part of Commercial Code came into effect in 1986 through the Accounting Directives Act ("Bilanzrichtliniengesetz"), which was instituted in compliance with the European Community law stipulating that the Fourth, Seventh and Eighth EC Directives be incorporated into national law.

Books and records must be kept in accordance with the principles of proper accounting ("Grundsätze ordnungsgemässer Buchführung"). These principles are derived from a variety of sources and are constantly being developed, expanded and interpreted. Requirements of the Commercial Code include:

- the maintenance of books and records in a modern language and the notation of currency figures in German Marks,
- the preparation of annual financial reports,
- the retention of account books, other financial records, invoices and correspondences for a certain prescribed period of time.

The tax laws require that the AG's accounting system be maintained in such a way that an independent expert can obtain an overview of its assets, liabilities and business operations within a reasonably short time. The account records must be kept and archived in Germany. Usually the company's goods must be inventoried and the results of the inventory recorded in the balance sheet with validity as of the date on which the balance sheet is legally due.

Further requirements contained in the HGB as well as the AktG regarding the preparation and presentation of financial reports include:

- maintenance and reflection in the balance sheet of a statutory reserve fund equal in amount to the value of at least ten per cent of the common stock,
- use of a prescribed format for the balance sheet and income statement,
- compliance with certain rules pertaining to the valuation of assets, liabilities, and stockholder equities; for example, the whole share capital must be stated at par value and liabilities must be indicated in terms of the amounts due,
- and compliance with specific depreciation rules.

The Commercial Code requires that the financial statements of mid-size and large stock corporations be audited by a Certified Public Accountant appointed by the stockholders. Following the audit, the accountant must issue an opinion whether the accounting system, the financial statements and the annual report comply with the law and the corporation's own articles of incorporation. In small stock corporations, the financial statements must be approved only by the supervisory board.

6. Liquidation

a) Reasons for dissolution

Stock corporations may be dissolved

- when a pre-planned period of existence set forth in the articles of association expires,
- upon decision of a three-forth majority of the voting stockholders
- or if an adjudication of bankruptcy is declared.

Further grounds for dissolution include:

- court denial of a bankruptcy petition stemming from its estimation that the corporation lacks enough assets to cover the costs of bankruptcy proceedings,
- a determination by the court of registry that a defect in the articles of incorporation exist
- or the corporation is uncapitalized.

The articles of incorporation may state yet further reasons and conditions under which the corporation is to be dissolved. When a ground for dissolution exists, the board of management must apply for the registration of the dissolution of the corporation in the commercial register.

The following extraordinary circumstances may also result in a formal end to the AG's existence:

- corporate merger ("Verschmelzung"),
- and the transformation of the AG into another type of business organization ("Umwandlung").

In contrast to the grounds for dissolution discussed above, however, the occurrence of one of these three types of extraordinary circumstances does not result in the liquidation of the AG, which continues to pursue its original purpose, albeit in another form.

b) Insolvency and liquidation

The liquidation procedure of an AG is clearly prescribed by law. Basically, two kinds of liquidation proceedings are recognized. When insolvency is the cause for the dissolution, the liquidation procedures to be followed are those set forth in the Bankruptcy Act ["Konkursordnung" (KO), Par. 207 f.]. This law grants special protections to creditors. For example, if the board of management determines that the losses of an AG exceed its stated capital or the corporation cannot meet its obligations because of insolvency, it must file a petition in bankruptcy with the local court within three weeks. Failure of the board to do so can make its members personally liable and subject to criminal prosecution. Creditors of the corporation also have the right to file a petition for its bankruptcy. The liquidators are appointed by the court. If insolvency is not the basis for the corporation's dissolution, the AG must be liquidated according to the procedures delineated in the Stock Corporation Law (Par. 264 AktG). In accordance with these procedures, the members of the board of management serve as liquidators unless the articles of incorporation or a resolution of the stockholders provide otherwise.

The liquidators have to advise creditors of the dissolution of the AG by way of a notice published three consecutive times in the required newspaper or periodical. In the notice they must clearly request that any and all creditors submit their claims. All creditor claims including those of the tax authorities must be settled before any of the corporation's assets can be distributed among its stockholders. The distribution of remaining assets cannot occur earlier than one year after the third public notice to the creditors. Once the liquidation is complete and the final financial statements have been prepared, the liquidators must apply for the entry of the closing of the corporation in the commercial register.

III. Partnership Forms of Business Organizations

A. Civil-law partnership ["Gesellschaft des bürgerlichen Rechts" (also referred to as "GbR" or "BGB-Gesellschaft")]

The civil-law partnership does not possess the status of a separate legal entity and is not registered in the commercial register. It must act, sue or be sued by naming all its members.

The GbR may not be used as the organizational form for a business which falls under the definition of a "Handelsgewerbe," or commercial trade enterprise owned and operated by individuals who are merchants by profession. It is most often used to govern relationships between several partners in a professional society engaged in the provision of professional services, such as a law office or any other group of independent professionals working in a joint office.

To form a GbR, at least two partners must enter into a partnership agreement ("Gesellschaftsvertrag"). This agreement need not be in writing, and the parties are usually free to agree to the terms they see fit, even if such terms are different from the provisions of the Civil Code (BGB) pertaining to this type of business. The law requires only that the partners agree to the purpose to be promoted and combine their efforts in pursuance of a common economic objective (Par. 705 BGB).

The assets of a GbR are held by all partners jointly ("Gesamthands-vermögen", i.e. "joint ownership"). The assets cannot be disposed of without agreement between all the partners (Par. 719 BGB). The partners cannot convey their membership and share of the assets to another person without the agreement of the other partners or unless provisions to the contrary were made in the partnership agreement.

All of the partners normally have the same rights. They jointly share in the profits and losses and equally participate in any liquidation proceedings. All partners have equal voting rights in the partnership meetings and are able to represent the partnership as a whole in their dealings with third parties only through joint participation of the other partners unless the partnership agreement provides for another form of representation. For example, if the partnership agreement so allows, the partners may appoint one or more managing partners and invest them with the authority to act on behalf of the partnership as a whole, according to the standard principles of representation, and to enter agreements with third parties that bind the company. According to the principle of self-organization, which applies here, a fully authorized manager must be a partner in the business.

The liability for obligations resulting from transactions conducted in the name of the partnership is carried by all the partners jointly and severally. Unless a contract with a given creditor provides otherwise, creditors with unsatisfied claims are entitled to sue the partners both as members of the GbR and as private individuals. In this manner, creditors can tap the assets of both the partnership and its individual members. Debtors of the partnership, however, may not set off any claims they might have against a single partner against their liability to the partnership as a whole.

B. General partnership ["Offene Handelsgesellschaft" (OHG)]

The Commercial Code ("Handelsgesetzbuch," or HGB) makes provisions for the establishment of a partnership among merchants who wish to pursue a common commercial purpose under a common name (Par. 105 HGB). That organizational form is the simplest among merchants engaged in trade and is the counterpart of the GbR -- it is to merchants what the GbR is to professionals. It can be chosen by merchants only, or by people who intend to operate a commercial trade ("Handelsgewerbe"). The Commercial Code (HGB) clearly defines what constitutes a commercial trade and what types of business endeavors can be organized as one.

The OHG is structured similarly to the GbR and is not a separate legal entity. The partners own the partnership property jointly ("Gesamthandsvermögen"), and all of the partners, or "general partners," are subject to personal liability for the company's debts (Par. 128 HGB). The partners may be natural persons or legal entities. A legal entity may be partner in an OHG, however, only if it is also engaged in merchant trading and corresponds in all respects to what the law defines as a "Handelsgewerbe."

Persons forming an OHG do so typically out of a desire to achieve a true co-partnership, to which the partners devote both their labor and financial resources. Normally each partner has the authority to act on behalf of the business and enter binding agreements in its name, which allows for flexible operations. The unlimited liability of all the partners, which is a mandatory characteristic of partnerships, improves the chances of these types of companies receiving bank credit if and when required.

The intense nature of the relationship of the partners in an OHG requires that each partner has confidence and trust in the reliability and abilities of the other partner(s). When such confidence and mutual trust are present, the OHG is a good form in which to organize a small or a mid-size enterprise.

The OHG comes into existence through its registration in the commercial register. Even in the event that it is not registered, however, and a creditor issues a claim against it, the courts will rule that an OHG does indeed exist if a partnership agreement has been entered into and a transaction with a third party has taken place. The general provisions of the Commercial Code (HGB) apply to partnership agreements unless they contain contrary terms which are allowed under the Commercial Code.

The general partnership must be filed in the commercial register in notarized form. The application for the filing of the OHG must include the name, address and occupation of each partner, the company name and location as well as the date on which business will be commenced. All the partners must submit specimen signatures.

The company name of an OHG must contain the name of at least one of the partners in addition to a clear designation of the company as a general partnership. (e.g. "Bernard Mueller OHG" or "Bernard Mueller & Co."). Descriptive additions to the name are admissible, but they cannot be either misleading or confusing. Any change in the company name or location or in the identity of its partners must be registered in the commercial register.

Although it is not a legal entity, a general partnership can sue and be sued (Par. 124 HGB). Thus, a creditor of the OHG may sue the partnership itself under the company name as well as each of the partners individually. A private creditor of one of the partners, however, cannot file suit against the OHG itself.

At the end of each business year, the managing partners must prepare a balance sheet and have it approved and signed by all of the partners. The partnership agreement may require that this annual statement of accounts be approved at a meeting of the partners and/or examined by a public accountant. An OHG, like all other business enterprises, is obliged to conduct proper bookkeeping in accordance with the regulations of the Commercial Code (HGB).

Under the Commercial Code, reasons for dissolution of an OHG include a unanimous resolution of the partners, bankruptcy or the death of one of the partners. The partners can stipulate in their agreement other conditions under which the company can be dissolved. Should the stipulated conditions arise, any of the partners has the right to initiate dissolution proceedings by way of regular notice.

In the event that circumstances arise which make it unreasonable for the partnership to continue in existence, the law provides for the possibility to give extraordinary notice and subsequently file for special legal action seeking a dissolution order (Par. 133 HGB). The partner's right to seek such an order under extraordinary conditions cannot be restricted in the partnership agreement. Regardless of the reason for dissolution, the partnership agreement may contain a provision which allows the remaining partners to perpetuate the business.

C. Limited partnership ["Kommanditgesellschaft" (KG)]

The KG is a special form of an OHG. It is also formed by merchant partners for the purpose of operating a commercial business enterprise under a single company name. The rules governing the OHG (Par. 105 ff. HGB) are generally applicable to the KG unless modified by subsequent provisions of the Commercial Code (Par. 161 ff. HGB).

The main and most important difference between an OHG and a KG is that the KG consists of two different kinds of partners: personally liable partners ("Komplementäre") and limited partners ("Kommanditisten"). As their designations clearly indicate, the personally liable partners are liable for the debts of the company without any limitation. Their rights and duties correspond to those of an OHG partner. Normally, because they devote their labor and are subject to greater financial risk, the personally liable partners are responsible for the company's management and representation. The liability of the limited partners, on the other hand, is limited to the amount of their capital investments in the partnership. These contributions can be cash, non-cash equivalents or even in the form of a substantiated claim against the company.

A KG must consist of at least one personally liable partner and at least one limited partner. Other rules regarding the KG's formation are similar to the requirements for the establishment of an OHG except that the different rights and duties of the two types of partners must be observed, particularly in the partnership agreement.

German law strictly differentiates between the external representation of a company and its internal management. As a rule, the power of the personally liable partners to represent the firm externally cannot be restricted to certain types of transactions or by general limitations. The only type of restriction which is effective vis à vis third parties is a joint-representation provision in the partnership agreement, which can provide either that the signatures of two or more personally liable partners is required in order to bind the KG or the signatures of two or more personally liable partners and the signature of another (such as a "Prokurist") is necessary before the KG is bound. A KG which wishes to be governed by such a provision must file an application for the entry of it in the commercial register.

While it is not possible to deprive the personally liable partners of their rights of representation and the corresponding right of third parties to rely on them (external management rights), just the opposite is true of the limited partners. Due to their limited liability, the limited partners are not entitled to represent the firm unless they have been granted a full power of attorney ("Prokura," or "Handlungsvollmacht").

With regard to the internal management of the KG, however, German law allows greater flexibility. For example, the partnership agreement may allocate certain types of responsibilities to different partners, exclude a partner completely from management or allow management participation of limited partners.

The obligation to prepare the annual balance sheet lies with the personally liable partners. However, the partnership agreement may also provide for the participation of the limited partners. A KG is subject to the same accounting, auditing and dissolution requirements as an OHG (see section B. above).

D. Silent partnership ("Stille Gesellschaft")

A silent partnership is formed by a partnership agreement. No registration or other disclosure is required. The silent partnership, therefore, remains a genuine internal affair between the silent partner and the principal who owns the business.

As a rule, the sole obligation of silent partners is to make a capital investment in accordance with the partnership agreement. Management rights are vested in the principal. Generally, silent partners have no more right to control the business than do the limited partners of a KG. Silent partners participate in the profits of the partnership, but usually do not share the losses. Silent partners usually have no claim to the hidden reserves of the business.

Silent partners are able to lay claim for repayment of their investments upon dissolution of the partnership. Unless the partnership agreement provides otherwise, silent partners possess the same rights as a creditors. This holds true even in the case of bankruptcy.

It is possible for the parties to agree that any silent partner(s) will participate in profits and losses upon liquidation and in the hidden reserves. Such an arrangement results in the creation of a "non-typical" silent partnership.

Foreign companies with German subsidiaries are often confronted with a situation in which their subsidiaries require additional funds. The silent partnership can be used to acquire such funds.

IV. Mixed Corporate / Partnership Organizational Forms

A. GmbH & Co. KG

The GmbH & Co. KG is a form that combines the limited liability company (GmbH) with a limited partnership (KG) and is frequently used in Germany. The advantage of this form of business organization is the fact that a GmbH may (and usually does) participate as the only personally liable partner of the KG, thus limiting the liability of the only personally liable partner. The GmbH can be held liable for its business debts only to the extent of its assets. Its liability cannot be extended to the private property of its shareholders. Therefore, there is no real unlimited liability of any of the partners in a GmbH & Co. KG.

When the GmbH is the sole personally liable partner, it has the duty of managing and representing the GmbH & Co. KG. The GmbH fulfills its responsibilities in this regard through the efforts of its own managing director(s).

B. Limited partnership with stock ["Kommanditgesellschaft auf Aktien" (KGaA)]

The KGaA is another mixed type of partnership / corporate form available for use in Germany. Though it is relatively rare, some of the largest enterprises in Germany have chosen to use it. It possess attributes of both a limited partnership as well as a stock corporation. Like a corporation, it is a separate legal entity. Yet like a limited partnership, at least one of its personally liable partners must bear the full liability for all the debts of the company. The other partners (limited stockholders) own stock in the company but are not personally liable to the company's creditors (Par. 278 AktG).

The limited stockholders are entitled to participate in the corporation's affairs only through concerted action taken at stockholder meetings. The personally liable partner(s) are responsible for the management and representation of the company.

V. Other Business Organizational Forms

A. Sole proprietorship ("Einzelunternehmen")

The sole proprietorship is one of the most popular organizational forms for small businesses due to the comparative ease with which it can be formed and operated. In general, a small merchant ("Minderkaufmann") is not required to register the proprietorship in the commercial register.

Sole proprietors, like the general partners of an OHG, are subject to personal liability for all the debts of the business. Consequently, their private assets can be impounded if necessary in order to satisfy the claims of creditors. If sole proprietors are engaged in the types of merchant trade listed in section 1 par. 1 of the Commercial Code (HGB), then they are considered to be operating "Handelsgewerbe" and must register the business.

B. Branch office ("Zweigniederlassung")

Instead of or in addition to the formation of a new enterprise, it is often advisable for a foreign company to set up a branch office ("Zweigniederlassung") in Germany. Tax advantages often play an important role in such a decision. The corporate income tax rate applied to the profits of a branch office are 46% compared to 50% for a subsidiary. On the other hand, a parent company is liable to the full extent of its own assets for creditors' claims filed against the branch.

A branch has no legal personality of its own and thus derives its rights and obligations from the status of the head office of the parent company. It may sue or be sued only through the parent company. By virtue of its local presence, however, a foreign company operating as a branch office in Germany can have action taken against it by any local creditor through the local judicial system.

German law makes a distinction between dependent and independent branches. If a branch can be considered to be a separate or independent entity, then it has to be registered in the commercial register (Par. 13 HGB). An independent branch can be established only if it has its own assets, bank accounts and bookkeeping system and would be able to continue in operation even if the head office were to close down. In addition, an independent branch must be represented by a manager who has the power to enter contracts and agreements that legally bind the branch. A smaller branch that cannot be considered to be self-supporting and independent need not be registered in the commercial register.

An independent branch may operate and be listed in the commercial register under its own company name. This name must consist of the name of the parent association and may contain an additional distinguishing term. The application for entry of the branch in the commercial register must be signed by all the officers of the company in the presence of a notary. Normally, their signatures must be submitted to the German consulate but, according to the Hague Convention of October 5th, 1961, this requirement can be met through the attachment of an "Apostille."

The application for registration must include the company's name, registered location and purpose in addition to a description of its financial basis and legal structure. Documents required in the application process must be notarized and accompanied by a German translation.

The founders of either type of branch office must notify the local Trade Supervision Office ("Gewerbeaufsichtsamt") in order to enable the authorities to determine whether a license is necessary or not. The notification is required by par. 14 of the Trade Supervision Law ["Gewerbeordnung" (GewO)]. Usually, no special license is required unless the branch's planned enterprise falls into a special category of business. Such special categories include, to cite the most common ones, banks, restaurants, hotels, bars, insurance companies and commercial transportation enterprises. Failure to provide the required notification can result in a substantial fine.

VI. Corporate Succession and Changes of Organizational Form

The business development of an AG, GmbH or KGaA can result in the need or desire for a transformation of the company ("Umwandlung"), a merger with at least one other corporation ("Verschmelzung durch Aufnahme") or a consolidation with another corporation for the purpose of forming a new corporation ("Verschmelzung durch Neubildung").

A. Merger and consolidation

A merger takes place under German law when the total assets and liabilities of one corporate enterprise are transferred to another in return for shares in it. As a result of a merger, the transferee company is terminated and its shareholders become shareholders in the acquiring corporation [i.e. merger by take over ("Verschmelzung durch Aufnahme")].

A consolidation occurs when the assets and liabilities of two or more corporations are transferred to a newly formed corporation in return for shares in this new corporation ("Verschmelzung durch Neubildung").

The following types of enterprises can be fused through either a merger or a consolidation:

- two or more stock corporations (AGs),
- two or more limited partnerships with stock (KGaAs)

- a stock corporation (AG) with a limited partnership with stock (KGaA)
- or two or more GmbHs.

A limited liability company (GmbH) can be fused with a stock corporation or a limited partnership with stock (KGaA) only through a merger (Par. 355 AktG

B. Transformation

In contrast to a merger or consolidation, a transformation impacts only one business by changing its organizational form. Under the provisions of the AktG, an AG may be transformed into either a GmbH or a KGaA and vice versa.

A transformation of an AG into a KGaA requires a resolution passed by a three-fourth majority vote of the stockholders. A transformation of an AG to a GmbH, however, generally requires the unanimous approval of all the voting stockholders. In the first case, the transformation must be approved by the personally liable partners.

To effect a transformation of a GmbH into an AG or a KGaA, the shareholders must approve an amendment of the articles of incorporation reflecting the change. An application must be made to have the names of the members of the board of management of the newly created stock corporation and the transformation itself noted in the commercial register. At the time the registration of the transformation occurs, the GmbH still continues to exist, though now in the form of the new company: a stock corporation (AG) or a limited partnership with stock (KGaA). The share capital becomes stock capital, and shares or ownership interests become stock.

Under the provisions of the Transformation Act ("Umwandlungsgesetz"), GmbHs, AGs, and KGaAs may be transformed into general partnerships (OHGs) or limited partnerships (KGs).

Chapter 2

THE ACQUISITION OF CLOSELY HELD COMPANIES

Bernd Tremml

I. Introduction

The basic reason behind the acquisition of a company is the same in all countries -- the purchaser wishes to acquire the value of another enterprise. As is obvious but too often forgotten, the legal system of the country where the purchase will take place has a considerable impact on the consummation of an acquisition. Of particular importance is the local corporate law, especially the provisions of it that govern business organizations and structures.

The structure as well as the content of the rules and regulations of German law may appear strange to a person more familiar with Anglo-American law. For example, in Germany, whenever parties have no written agreement on a particular issue, the law, as it is interpreted by the courts, will apply or impose a solution. Thus, a party that might have forgotten to address a particular issue does not remain completely unprotected.

Such judicially imposed contract terms are, however, often viewed as very unsatisfactory by either the purchaser or seller of a business enterprise. In the absence of an agreement to the contrary, the law holds the seller liable only in disputes of material significance, which shifts the weight of risk in all other cases to the shoulders of the purchaser. To clarify matters from the onset and avoid such judicial impositions as well as the hassles and high costs of litigation, it has meanwhile become common practice for the parties in an acquisition transaction to agree to specific terms that are within the range of the law and clearly lay them out in the form of a written contract.

An acquisition involves such diverse areas of law as contract, commercial, corporate, labor, and tax law and sometimes even inheritance or domestic-relations law. Through a contract, the laws can be tailored to meet the needs of a specific case, which offers both the seller and purchaser considerably better protection. It is imperative that significant attention be focused on the drafting of the acquisition contract.

II. Types of Acquisition

As discussed in the previous chapter, German law provides for a variety of business organizational forms, which can be divided into sole proprietorships, partnerships, corporations and forms that are a mixture of the latter two. Only a relatively small number of German companies issue stock and trade it on the open market. As mentioned, the stock corporation (AG) is chosen by only a handful of large and mainly international enterprises, and because its stock is freely traded, there is nothing its management can do to prevent a purchaser bent on acquiring a majority of stocks from getting them. Therefore, in terms of acquisition, it has a unique status. All the other types of enterprises are customized to meet the needs of their owners, and as a general rule, their equity holdings are not openly traded or even freely transferable. They can therefore be described as privately or closely held enterprises. This chapter will deal primarily with the acquisition of GmbHs, the legal form of a closely held company that is most commonly chosen by mid-sized German enterprises.

There are two ways in which to acquire any kind of already existing German enterprise: the acquisition of ownership interests (the equity holdings of a GmbH or the stock of an AG, for instance) or the acquisition of all or some of its assets and liabilities. In either of these ways, an enterprise can be acquired in whole or in part.

A. Acquisition of ownership interests

As a rule, all the rights of ownership are transferred from the seller of a GmbH to the buyer on the date of purchase. It's important to know exactly what that entails.

Prior to the acquisition, an interim balance sheet must be prepared, which shows the expected profits to the date of sale, as of which the equity holdings of the GmbH together with the right to receive future profits are transferred to the buyer. Any necessary adjustments to the interim balance sheet must be made in accordance with the final financial report.

B. Sale of assets

The sale of assets is quite complex because a great degree of specificity is required and detailed attention must be given to the matter to avoid the possibility of error. Each item of property, as well as all the rights and liabilities associated with it, needs to be accurately and clearly listed in the acquisition agreement.

1. Real estate

The conditions of ownership and a detailed description of any real estate property can be conclusively determined from the information contained in the real estate register. Buildings constitute an integral part of the real estate. Appurtenances such as machines are included in the sale of real estate unless otherwise agreed. The transfer to the purchaser occurs when an agreement by both the seller and the purchaser has been entered into before a German notary public and the transfer has been officially noted in the real estate register.

2. *Purchase of current moveable assets or groups of moveable assets*

If current moveable assets or groups of moveable assets are sold, the individual items must be accurately and clearly listed in the acquisition agreement. With groups of assets, a purely quantitative description (i.e. "100 units") is not sufficient. Assets must be identified according to time and place, which is achieved by applying the so-called "All-Formula" rule in such a manner as to signify for example that all the items located in a particular stockroom or warehouse on the date of purchase will be conveyed to the purchaser.

Current moveable assets and groups of moveable assets are often encumbered by third-party security rights. It is important to treat such items separately in the agreement since they could, of course, be excluded from the transfer. However, it can also be agreed that the sellers' right to have such an item released or conveyed to them upon satisfaction of the claim for which it was offered as security, is transferred to the purchaser. The transfer of title to movable objects is effected by conveyance; or, if a third party is in possession of the object, by surrender of the right to possession.

3. Claims

Claims can be transferred if it is possible to substantiate them, for example, through a designation of the underlying transaction or the name of the debtor. If the purchaser intends to continue to operate the business of the seller after acquisition of it, the designation "all claims of the seller resulting from operations of the business" effectively serves the purpose. Such claims then become the enforceable claims of the purchaser. To avoid unpleasant surprises, the purchaser should, as in the case of the purchase of movable objects described above, insist on a detailed record of all outstanding claims. As a further security measure, the purchaser should obtain a personal guarantee from the seller that those claims will be satisfied by the seller in the event of default.

4. Company name and special industrial property rights

A company name can be transferred along with the sale of the company as a whole. The express agreement of the seller is, however, necessary for the continued use of the company name by the purchaser. Applications for change of registration and notarized transfer registrations should be made at the time of the closing of the sale.

Patents can be transferred separately, and as a rule they are transferred whenever the assets of the firm are transferred as a whole. If the rights resulting from a patent or design should need to be asserted against a third party, the transfer must have been previously registered. Often patents or designs are registered in the name of the previous owner. Therefore, verification is indispensable.

5. Additional rights and obligations

All remaining rights and obligations, any contracts which are to be assumed and any intangible assets such as know-how, customers, good will and so on should be listed in as accurate a manner as possible. When the transfer of a right is not regulated by applicable law, the pertinent details must be agreed upon. Also, the extent of any corresponding guarantees and indemnities of the seller should be set forth as clearly as possible in the sale's contract because they may be a purchaser's only recourse in case of a failure in the transfer of any such right. Of course, an accurate description of the right or obligation also serves to provide a dependable basis for the calculation of the purchase price. Because the transfer of a contract containing an assumption of debt requires the agreement of the creditor, a three-party agreement among the seller, the purchaser and the creditor will have to be made, or consent of the creditor to the transfer will otherwise have to be secured.

III. Contract Formalities

A. Letter of intent, negotiation contracts and preliminary contracts

1. Liability during contract negotiations

Acquisition contract negotiations cost both time and energy. Expenses prior to and in anticipation of the execution of the contract are often incurred, and more often than not business secrets are revealed. Thus, the question arises how the relationship between the parties should be regulated during the preliminary stages of contract negotiations.

As a general rule, negotiations alone do not obligate the parties to enter into a acquisition contract. In theory, the negotiations can be broken off without any justifiable reason, and it is possible to engage in parallel negotiations with other parties. Nonetheless, the law imposes a fiduciary relationship between the negotiating parties, which obliges them to observe and respect the just interests of the other.

A foreign purchaser may be surprised that even before any contractual obligations are incurred, a negotiating partner is liable for damages in accordance with the rules of *culpa in contrahendo* (anticipatory breach). For example, if a potential purchaser makes personal use of a business secret that he or she becomes aware of during the course of negotiations, he or she is liable for any damages. Also, even in the absence of any intent to cause a loss, if a purchaser or a seller breaks off the negotiations, they may be liable for damages the other party sustains through "detrimental reliance." Such damages might be, for instance, the irreversible expenditures the other party incurred through relying on the probable execution of the contract, expenditures which, upon the breaking off of the contract negotiations, constitute a definite loss.

2. Letter of intent and negotiation contracts

German business practice uses a letter of intent as part of preliminary contract negotiations. According to German law, such a letter is in principle a pure declaration of intent. It is meant to preclude adverse legal consequences and not to obligate a party to execute a final contract, even if a party states that under certain circumstances it is willing to be bound to do so. It should be noted, however, that the negotiating parties may rely on the probable execution of a final contract if the wording of the letter of intent seems to assume that a final contract will be entered into. The possibility of liability for reliance injury is obvious in such a case.

In order to preclude the risk and uncertainty of being sued for damages based on "detrimental reliance" in the event the contract negotiations are terminated, it is highly advisable to contractually determine the relationship the parties will have during the negotiation stage.

A preliminary agreement can include certain performance or disclosure obligations and/or a unilateral obligation on the part of the seller not to conduct any negotiations with third parties up to a certain point in time (according to German law, such a unilateral obligation is enforceable without the providing of consideration by the purchaser). The parties' agreement regarding their obligations during the negotiation stage can be laid out in the letter of intent.

However, a letter of intent which is used this way and contains provisions concerning certain performance or other obligations during the on-going contract negotiations, constitutes a binding offer to perform in accordance with the obligations. Its acceptance results in a so-called negotiation contract. Thus, in this way the parties can, for example, agree to and be bound by the following obligations:

- performance obligations (such as the conduction of preliminary investigations, marketing and location analyses, duty of disclosure),
- disclosure obligations (such as balance sheet audit, disclosure by designated employees),
- secrecy obligations (agreement not to use acquired information to one's own or to a third party's advantage),

- obligations pertaining to liability for omissions and reimbursement for expenses (including expert opinions, attorney fees, etc.)
- and obligations regarding dispute resolution (choice-of-law clause for the preliminary contract negotiations and arbitration agreements).

It is very important that the negotiation contract state whether these obligations are to remain in effect after the execution of the acquisition contract or whether they are to be extinguished by or integrated into the provisions of the acquisition contract.

It should be mentioned that the involvement of a broker (in practice often banks) can serve the secrecy requirements of the seller as well as the purchaser. A broker's professional expertise can furthermore be of great advantage to the prospective purchaser.

3. Preliminary contracts

When the basic terms regarding the acquisition contract are settled, a preliminary contract can be entered into even if certain issues still require further clarification. Such a preliminary agreement will impose an obligation on the parties to enter into a final acquisition contract.

B. Requirements of form

As a general rule, a contract for the sale of a partnership (other than a GmbH & Co. KG) which does not involve the transfer of real property need not conform to a specific form or meet specific legal requirements other than those pertaining to the enforceability of contracts in general. Contracts regulating the sale of all the assets and equity holdings of a GmbH, however, must conform to specific legal requirements.

The GmbH law (GmbHG) requires that the sale and transfer of equity holdings of such a company be effected by a German notary public ("Notar"). A "Notar" is a person who has the same training as an attorney but who acts impartially in a quasi-governmental function. A "Notar" must be involved in the transfer of the holdings of a GmbH regardless of whether their sale amounts to a partial or whole transfer of ownership.

If the contract is void because the special notarization requirements of the GmbH law have not been met, the purchaser has the right to be reimbursed in an amount equal to the sales price already paid. That right stems from the principle of unjust enrichment. The purchaser, however, will have to refund any profits obtained from the company if he or she knew or was grossly negligent in failing to realize that the contract was void.

Merger agreements through which an AG or GmbH transfers its assets as a whole to another corporation (merger by amalgamation) or by which several corporations or closely held companies such as a GmbH transfer their assets to a new corporation (merger by consolidation), need to be notarized and require compliance with the applicable statutes. Among other requirements, both companies must have their principal place of business within the Federal Republic of Germany. In practice, however, mergers are extremely rare.

IV. Specific Sale Considerations

A. Pending litigation

Upon the acquisition of the equity holdings of a GmbH, the company remains party to all on-going litigation and liable for any judgment. In order to avoid conflicts key points such as the following should be settled in an acquisition agreement:

- the seller should represent whether any, and what kind of, suits are pending (and what type of litigation is to be expected according to the best of his or her knowledge),
- the seller and purchaser should jointly defend ongoing suits, subject to their agreement concerning the nature and extent of each of their obligations,
- the parties should determine whether, depending on the outcome of pending litigation, the object of dispute will be re-transferred to the seller and, taking that prospect into account, make the necessary adjustments in the purchase price
- and the parties should reach an agreement concerning the right of either of them to appeal, recognize, settle, or dismiss actions and determine which one of them will be liable for the legal costs involved.

B. Legal liability of the purchaser for obligations

When the purchaser acquires the equity holdings of a GmbH, the GmbH as a legal entity remains liable for its existing obligations. Personal liabilities of either the seller or purchaser or both can nevertheless arise. Sellers are liable, for instance, if they have fallen into arrears in their payments of the original capital investment or in their fulfillment of additional service obligations.

Seller and purchaser will be jointly liable, according to their proportionate share holdings, for any overdue obligations to the GmbH which were not satisfied by other owners.

Needless to say, in any case the purchaser must have full knowledge of and access to the GmbH documents

("Gesellschaftsverträge") which clearly define the rights of the owners and their financial obligations.

C. Labor law requirements

The complexity and impact of German labor law on business operations tends to cause potential foreign investors serious concerns and may in fact prevent a successful acquisition.

Purchasers typically desire to retain those employees needed for a successful perpetuation of the company's business activities, and it is important that they take the proper steps in doing so. If a previously independent company is incorporated into a larger business structure, the loss of autonomous decision-making power often encourages management and executive personnel to resign.

On the other hand, there are cases in which company purchasers have the legal obligation to assume existing employee relationships although they may have no interest in doing so or may wish to change the relationships. This might occur, for instance, when someone acquires stock or equity holdings in a company. Employee relationships remain unchanged in that case as there was no actual change of employer. Since German labor laws have such an enormous impact on business operations, it is essential that potential foreign purchasers familiarize themselves with the laws and their implications.

Germany has very clearly spelled out employee-dismissal regulations, and there is only a limited number of legally recognized conditions under which employment can be terminated. Its labor laws also include special protection measures for employees based on age, seniority, maternity or the presence of a handicap. These employee-friendly laws may seem as unusual and surprising to foreign purchasers as the obligations employers have under certain circumstances to continue making wage payments to employees on leaves of absence. The high degree of German employee protection, insurance, vacation and other benefits tends to cause initial astonishment, as does the fact that German labor laws grant employees the right to participate in company management and co-determine its policies. These issues will be dealt with in Chapter 5.

Upon becoming the new owner of an enterprise, a purchaser automatically assumes from a legal perspective all the employment relationships that currently exist in the enterprise. It should also be noted that employees have the right to object to a transfer of their employment aggreement to the new owner. If their objections are sustained, the seller will remain the employer. The purchaser is liable for all of the overdue wages owed to employees who are still in the company's retention at the time of acquisition. The seller and purchaser are jointly liable for all obligations which accrued prior to the acquisition and are due within a year after the transfer. Thus, the seller and purchaser have to regulate such liability between themselves in the form of a contract. For the most part, however, only the seller is liable for the claims of any employees who resigned prior to the acquisition. The purchaser needs to be aware of potential exceptions to that rule. Following a successful acquisition, the purchaser also becomes liable for vested interests in retirement payments and the pension commitments the company has made to its employees.

German labor laws grant employees special protection rights in the event of an acquisition. Their employment cannot be terminated as a direct result of it, which is to say that terminations stemming from the transfer of a company from one owner to another are legally prohibited. The termination of personnel following an acquisition is allowed only within restriction; for example, if restructuring plans were already in place at the time of the sale and there are objective reasons why the personnel affected by them cannot continue to be employed. The law also provides that upon acquisition the existing terms of collective-bargaining agreements and the existing wage-and-salary structures continue to be valid and binding. They cannot be changed if that would have an adverse effect on the employees, whose interests, by law, cannot be limited or abridged as the consequence of an acquisition.

It is ,furthermore, important to note that as the result of an acquisition or merger a company's employees might gain the right to be represented on certain of its administrative boards. If, as a result of the sale, the company now employs more than 2,000 people, the right of employee participation in management comes into effect. The company must provide for employee representation on the supervisory board ("Aufsichtsrat").

In sum, the necessity of pre-sale legal review of all the labor-law issues and implications involved in an acquisition cannot be underscored too strongly. A potential purchaser should be well informed about the legal situation and take the necessary measures of protection in advance of purchase in order to avoid costly, never-ending future litigation (see Chapter 5).

D. Breach of contract

It is of particular importance to a purchaser to know what the legal outcome will be if the actual assets of a business enterprise were incorrectly represented in the purchase agreement or if the enterprise does not develop as projected and described in the agreement. If no contract provisions address these issues, then the following prevails:

Because the sale of stock or equity holdings is an effective legal transaction, sellers are liable only for the legality of the ownership interests. That is to say, they are not responsible for the conditions of whatever it is the ownership interests entitle their holders to (the assets of a company). The purchasers of stock or equity holdings are protected by law only when they in effect acquire the entire enterprise. Yet even in that case, the seller can be held liable only for the lack of those assets whose absence would undermine the very existence of the enterprise as whole. For example, a seller would be liable for a material deficiency that might exist in discrepancy to the capital asset account. The seller, however, is not generally liable for any incorrect statements concerning sales, profits and profitability or the total amount of the existing liabilities. Prospective purchasers are therefore well advised to demand specific warranties from the seller of a business, and this in writing, as their chances of holding the seller liable for any statements, indications or promises would otherwise be very weak indeed. A written warranty, however, would serve as a court-recognized basis for proving deception and/or damage and make it possible to tag an appropriate monetary figure to it. This warranty should be an integral part of the attorney-prepared purchase contract if it is to have the full potential to stand up in court.

Since purchasers of closely held companies are at a relative disadvantage to the sellers and since there is a great deal of ambiguity concerning their rights and obligations in general, it is highly recommended that all unclear and open issues be resolved in writing. In how much detail the various issues ought to be treated depends largely on the negotiating parties. However, the minimum to be obtained from the seller should be a guarantee concerning the net assets and profits of the enterprise. It should include attests to past business performance and to existing or non-existing transactions as well as to realistically projected future developments. In conjunction with such an agreement, the form and extent of the seller's liability should be agreed upon.

The seller should also guarantee that the balance sheet is complete and accurate, was prepared in accordance with the proper, legally proscribed accounting principles, and will be updated by way of supplement if necessary. The parties should also make an agreement as to what independent certified public accountants will verify the balance sheet. Procedures for any necessary adjustments of the purchase price should also be clearly laid out. The seller should be asked to provide warranties regarding the firm's inventory, hidden reserves, high-risk transactions and sale restrictions as well as warranties pertaining to the validity of any operating permits and licenses. The statement procured from the seller should also contain mention of any provisions governing the transfer of know-how and any restrictions, geographical and otherwise, on competition. Such restrictions may also apply to the prior owner's right to use his or her name in another business. The seller's obligations to disclose pending litigation and other liabilities can be supported by a guarantee that the information was provided to the best of the seller's ability and knowledge.

A mechanism should also be in place for establishing the liability of the seller and determining the type and extent of damage for which the seller is responsible. It is to the advantage of both parties to agree to a purchase price reduction rather than to the purchaser's right to rescind a sale in the event that the seller becomes liable for certain damage. Provisions for the right to rescind a sale should be made only in the most extreme cases. It is also general practice to extend the standard one-year duration of warranty obligations to two years by way of written agreement.

E. Expenses

Expenses incurred through the acquisition of an enterprise should be covered in the agreement. Attorney and notary public fees are legally fixed in Germany. The amount is determined according to the value of the matter in question. In the case of a whole-company acquisition, the value of the company determines the amount of the legal fees. When stock or equity holdings are being transferred, the legal fees are based on either the total nominal capital or the purchase price of the holdings. If individual assets such as real estate are being sold, the fees are based on the assets' current market value. For example, if the acquisition price of the equity holdings of a closely held corporation such as a GmbH is DM 500,000.--, the attorney will be entitled to up to DM 15,000--, and the notary public who certifies the sales contract and the assignment of the equity holdings will be entitled to DM 2,500. Variation in these fees is allowed in individual cases; usually attorneys charge in acquisition cases hourly fees, ranging from DM 350.00 to DM 700.00. Further expenses include the costs for the registration of the equity holdings in the commercial register or, in the case of the transfer of real estate, in the real-estate register. Those fees are comparatively lower.

V. Restrictions

A. Restrictions on sale

Prospective purchasers should make themselves aware of any restrictions the seller might have on the rights to sell the object in question. If any restrictions exist, the sales contract could be void or ineffective until the necessary approvals have been granted. Special areas such as family (domestic relations) and inheritance law, will not be considered here, although they may be of high impact and should not be overlooked when considering a purchase.

The purchaser of an enterprise has to know who is authorized to effect its sale. The sale or merger of an AG cannot be agreed to by the board of management or supervisory board alone, but requires the consent of a qualified majority of the stockholders at a general meeting. Such consent can be dispensed with only if a part of the enterprise is being sold and the corporation can continue its activities in conformity with its existing articles of corporation. In the case of the sale of a GmbH or other closely held corporation, it is not clear whether the power of a managing director is sufficient to effect the transfer of the company or whether a meeting of owners must be called and a resolution authorizing the transfer adopted by a qualified majority. Thus, it is advisable to insist on such a resolution. It should be noted that the transfer of ownership interests of a closely held corporation can be restricted by the articles of incorporation, and the transfer can be made subject to the consent of the other owners.

B. Antitrust regulations

A prospective purchaser must be aware of the applicable antitrust regulations. These can apply to the acquisition of an entire enterprise or to the acquisition of only a partial interest in one. There is either a notification or a registration requirement. The acquisition of all of the assets of the enterprise or of an essential part of them is subject at least to compliance with the applicable notification provisions. The acquisition of shares of stock or equity holdings of a company is subject to such notification compliance if the ownership interests in question together with any interests already owned constitute a prescribed percentage of the voting stock or holdings. It can be as low as 25%. However, the duty of notification is triggered only if the combined firms have at least a 20% market share, DM 500 million in yearly sales or 10,000 employees. The duty of registration is triggered if one of the firms participating in the sale of ownership interest or assets has at least DM 2,000 million in world-wide yearly sales or if two or more of the participating firms had at least DM 1,000 million each in world-wide sales in the last complete business year.

In satisfying the notification requirements, the Federal Cartel Authority ("Bundeskartellamt") must be notified immediately after the sale. If the Federal Cartel Authority subsequently determines that the sale violates market control provisions (and determines that the acquisition does not qualify for an exception), it can prohibit the transaction within one year after the sale, and in such a case it will allow the parties an appropriate period of time to undo the transaction. If a sale of ownership interests or assets must comply with the more burdensome registration requirements of the Federal Cartel Authority, registration must occur prior to the closing of the sale. The Federal Cartel authority then has a period of four months in which to prohibit the transfer. The antitrust regulations must be examined closely on a case-by-case basis.

C. European Community regulations

The non-European purchaser must realize that the European Economic Community Treaty contains its own antitrust regulations and that ordinances and decisions of the Council and the Commission can be directly binding on individual parties within the Member States (see Chapter 9).

VI. Special Considerations for Foreign Purchasers

A. No basic restrictions

Basically, there are no restrictions on the acquisition of German companies by foreign purchasers. The transfer of assets or the acquisition of ownership interests by foreign investors can be prohibited only when this is necessary to protect the national interest, which is, for example, the case when armament control is involved. An acquisition can also be prohibited if an attempt is made to use it as a means of circumventing restrictions on the employment of foreigners not holding German residence permits.

B. Transfer of shares and assets

German international property law does not permit a choice of law as to the actual transfer of property, whether it is personal property or real estate. The transfer of a German company through the sale of assets or ownership interests must therefore take place in accordance with German law. The acquisition of ownership rights in German companies by foreigners is furthermore subject to the company's own articles of incorporation, which are governed by local laws. Thus, it is necessary to ascertain whether a stockholder or owner agreement or the corporate charter imposes any prohibitions.

VII. Tax Aspects for the Purchaser

A. Non-recurrent taxes incurred through the purchase of a business enterprise.

1. Value-added tax (VAT) ["Mehrwertsteuer" (MwSt.)

When a business enterprise is acquired in its entirety, such a purchase is subject to value-added tax(VAT). The purchaser(s) must pay the VAT to the entrepreneur selling the enterprise. In most cases they can deduct this amount as a pre-tax payment from their own tax debt; there is, however, a certain time lapse between payment and reimbursement of the value-added tax (usually at least one month). Purchasers definitely need to take this into account when drawing up their liquidity plans. A transfer of an entire business exists when the property transferred represents the fundamental and basic essentials of the business and at the same time will provide the fundamental and basic essentials of the new business (it is important to note that it is not necessary that all the property of the company change hands). Furthermore, the property must be transferred to one and the same purchaser, and this purchaser must be or become an entrepreneur as defined by the German Value-Added Tax Act. The German VAT rate is currently 15%; the basis of assessment are all outlays the purchaser made in accordance with the agreement in order to gain possession of the business enterprise. Assumptions of any debts cannot be deducted from this amount. It is, however, important to note that when the value-added tax is figured, the total sales price must be broken down into separate prices for each of the purchased assets. The list may include single items that can be transferred tax-free, such as holdings of equity capital, open accounts, monetary funds, securities or real estate that may be contained in the business property. If the sales price includes payment for the goodwill of the company, this is subject to the full value-added tax.

2. Real-estate acquisitions tax ("Grunderwerbssteuer")

In 1983, a new Real-Estate Acquisitions Tax Act came into effect in Germany, which has considerably simplified the legal situation. Most of the complicated and involved exemption regulations were deleted. The tax rate is now a uniform 3.5%. Frequently overlooked, however, is the fact that liability for the real-estate acquisitions tax can be incurred in ways other than through a simple purchase of real-estate property. Certain transactions under corporate law, such as those occurring upon the acquisition or merger of enterprises, may also be subject to this tax.

B. Liability for tax debts of the acquired enterprise

The legal liability of the purchaser for the indebtedness of an acquired company was discussed above. It should be pointed out here that those liability regulations generally apply to any tax debts as well. Art. 75 of the German Tax Code ["Abgabenordnung" (AO)] contains the following further provisions concerning tax liability:

- If the ownership of a business enterprise or a separately run company within the structure of a business enterprise is transferred in its entirety, the purchaser is liable for any taxes that have been incurred as a result of operating the business. . .;

> provided such taxes have come into existence within the period of one year after registration of the company by the purchaser. The liability is limited to the inventory of the acquired assets. . . .This does not apply to acquisitions from a bankrupt estate. . . or to acquisitions in the course of an executor process.

The purchaser is liable only for taxes that have been previously incurred in the process of operating the business. They would primarily include value-added tax and business taxes but not, however, such taxes as any income or corporate tax owed by the proprietors or shareholders of the company.

The sales contracts for business enterprises contain in most cases an agreement that all of the debts of the acquired enterprise that have been incurred up to the date of the signing of the contract will not be assumed by the purchaser but will remain the sole responsibility of the seller. Such a liability-exemption clause, while enforceable between the parties, does not exempt the purchaser from tax liability under German law. The liability claim established by section paragraph 75 of the Tax Code falls under the domain of public law and therefore cannot be excluded by private agreement. At the most, such a private agreement would simply provide the purchaser with a basis for claiming indemnity from the seller. If the seller is economically strong and within the reach of the tax authorities, however, it is possible in most cases to arrange with the revenue service that it continue making its claims directly to the previous owner.

It is of prime importance to purchasers that they avail themselves of the liability exemption provision of section 75, par. 1 of the German Tax Code by registering their company with the revenue office of their district, thereby triggering the running of the one year period. This is even more important in light of the fact that the purchasers' tax liability does not depend on whether or not they have knowledge of any existing tax debts.

The liability for the tax debts of the former or current owner is an area requiring extreme caution and care. Potential purchasers should consult with the tax authorities ("Finanzamt") to obtain all information pertaining to the tax situation of the seller.

C. Utilization of losses

If the acquired business enterprise has tax losses (as is frequently the case), the following provision should be considered:

- The German revenue tax laws allow for carrying losses back to previous years or forward to subsequent years. Up to ten million German Marks in losses that cannot be covered by positive income in the year of their origination are first carried back two years and deducted there. If deduction is not possible there either, the losses may be carried over to the year immediately preceding the assessment time period and deducted in that year. The tax notices received for those years will be revised by the tax authorities accordingly. If and when the losses exceed a total amount of ten million German Marks or if the total amount of them cannot be fully deducted by carrying them backwards to the two preceding years, then they can be carried forward and deducted over the next years.

This system of loss deduction, however, does not apply to "bare-shell" purchases of inactive limited private companies. If a limited private company (GmbH) which has excessive indebtedness or is ready to be liquidated is acquired simply as a "bare-shell" under the assumption that the deductible losses are valuable, the German tax law precedent rulings do not recognize the purchaser's claims to these losses.

Therefore, if the business enterprise that is to be acquired is currently in debt, it is of decisive importance to consult a tax advisor before the purchase is made. Prior to purchase it is still possible to try to cover losses that are impending or already have been incurred. One possibility would be, for example, the activation of idle reserves by selling single assets (perhaps by selling them in advance to the future purchaser of the business). Other possibilities would be discontinuing the increase of pension provisions and other special contingency reserves, immediately writing off the total cost of low-value goods, liquidating reserve funds on the basis of altered risk calculations as well as making expedient use of accounting options.

It is, of course, at all times necessary to make sure that no mandatory regulations of the commercial or tax laws are violated; otherwise, these alteration procedures may be completely or partially denied recognition, for instance, on the basis of misuse, concealed deposits or violation of the arm's-length-principle of German foreign tax laws.

VIII. Tax Benefits and other Incentives in the Acquisition of a Business Enterprise.

Before acquiring a business enterprise in the Federal Republic of Germany, investors should look into the types of financial backing and the special tax advantages *(for example, the investment incentive program)* that are available for their planned investment. Since regional differences in a federal country such as Germany can exist, it is very important for investors to have reliable consultants who are not only familiar with the promotional programs available for specific investment projects but also have good contacts with the regional authorities in charge of administering them. The promotional measures and special tax advantages available can change very quickly.

In order to support the investment in certain economic regions and especially in less developed regions of the country, many types of funds are made available by the Federal Government as well as by the Federal States.

These are mainly grants, allowances, beneficial interest rate loans and the provision of security bonds, guarantees and other securities.

Recently, these programs have been mainly designed to encourage investment in the new Federal States because this is the territory where it is most needed.

Furthermore, credit with low interest rates is available in order to encourage investments in the East German States. Such credit is mainly given to entrepreneurs who are just getting started in their own business in order to increase their capital resources.

In addition, the European Community provides support measures by the way of the European Investment Bank (EIB), the European Community for Coal and Steel (ECCS) and the European Regional Development Fund.

The EIB provides loans and guarantees in so far as they are appropriate to investment projects which contribute to the support of a balanced regional development as well as to the modernization and reconstruction of companies in the interest of the Community.

IX. Conclusion

The German civil-law system offers potential business purchasers considerably more protection than the Anglo-American common-law system offers them. They are nonetheless, well advised to seek a well thought out written agreement, which will enable them to make more informed business decisions and help them avoid future conflicts. This chapter does not contain a complete description of all the legal and tax issues that might arise in the acquisition of a company. Prospective purchasers are emphatically advised to rely on their own attorneys and tax consultants when preparing to make such a complicated transaction. Though as a general rule, it is always highly advisable to seek professional, individual help before acting on any decisions that could be of considerable economic impact, this holds particularly true in any issues involving taxes. German tax laws are constantly being revised. It is therefore essential that the current validity of the information presented here be verified, modified or adapted to a particular case by professionals who are abreast of the developments in the German tax-law arena before any binding commitments are made on the basis of it."

Acquisition-Agreement Checklist

Below, in the form of a checklist, are the essential issues which should be negotiated and included in an acquisition contract:

1) Parties

- including authorized representatives and persons with full powers of attorney

2) Preamble

- Motives and basis of the transaction

3) Object of sale

- acquisition of shares or assets
- Purchase of shares: special clause for the transition of loan accounts
- Sole proprietorships / partnerships: special clause for the transition of special equities. Reference to balance sheet and/or itemized listing of assets (indispensable when the object of sale is a part of the business)
- due diligence
- Special consideration: seller's right to withdraw capital to the date of closure
- Special consideration: seller's obligation to balance losses shown in the cash accounts or special accounts

4) Assumption of liabilities

- Acquisition of shares in the business: no specifications
- Acquisition of an enterprise: regulation of liabilities to the date of closure
- Acquisition of part of an enterprise: categorized itemization of assets
- Right of indemnity for non-assumed liabilities

5) Transition of employee relationships

- Enterprise as a whole: no specification required. Automatic regulation by Par. 613a BGB. Right of recision potentially possible in the event of employee objections
- Part of an enterprise: itemized categorization of employee relationships

6) Pension obligations

- Internal division of the pension obligations (no effect on employees)
- Transfer of support obligations to an independent relief fund
- Seller's termination obligation prior to transition
- Any hiring of new employees prior to closure requires purchaser approval

7) Current Contracts

- Purchaser approval
- Rights of indemnity

8) Personal securities

9) Unanticipated liabilities

- Warranty that all liabilities are included in the balance sheet
- Division of risk: obligation to indemnify, reduction of purchase price, set-off claims

10) Further declarations and regulations regarding:

- Contracts with advisors
- Division of sales and profits
- Security rights
- Long- term delivery contracts
- Pending transactions (division of future profits and losses)
- Approved cartels
- Currently existing non-competition agreements
- Currently existing powers of attorney
- Legal disputes

11) Permits under public law

- Warranty that the assets of the firm are unencumbered and its operations unendangered

12) Prohibition of competition

- Scope in terms of content, time and place

13) Determination of purchase price

- Determination criteria
- Basis for the determination of book values
- Quota-share regulation in the case of partial purchases
- Differences based on increase / reduction of current assets or short-term accounts receivable/accounts payable up to closure
- Right of indemnity for later payments decreasing the value of the firm, e.g. taxes
- Balance at transition: cooperation duties, valuation criteria, choice of CPAs including arbitrator

14) Warranties

- Completeness of all information provided
- Correctness of statements according to the best of knowledge
- Balance: continuation of current practices, no incurring of new liabilities
- Sales and profits: express assurance is necessary to hold the seller liable
- Exclusion of any rights to recision
- Reversal of transaction: maximum liability, secrecy obligations

15) Actual transition

- Exact point in time

- Method of transition (physical, assignment, transfer of trademarks, obtaining of records, etc.)
- Assurance that no essential changes have taken place between the time of contract and sale
- Methods of payment of the purchase price
- Purchaser's obligation to close (provided no essential changes have occurred and all pre-agreed conditions have been fulfilled)

16) General Regulations

- Duties of disclosure after sale
- Assurance that no illegal antitrust agreements exist
- Right to purchase further stock or equity holdings in the enterprise
- Choice of law
- Assumption of expenses (attorney, notary, commercial register, real-estate register)
- Division of taxes
- Jurisdiction
- Rescue clause

17) In the case of antitrust notification requirements:

- receipt of permission as a condition for suspension

18) Statute of Limitations

- for warranty claims
- for tax indemnity claims

19) Arbitration clause

Chapter 3

VALUATION OF BUSINESS ENTERPRISES

Bernd Tremml

I. General Information

The purchase of a business enterprise or shares of stock in one generally does not occur until the value of the business has been appraised. And the question as to what method should be used in determining the value of a business enterprise was vehemently disputed in Germany for a long time.

The method that had traditionally been employed for years and is now generally known as the „Stuttgart Procedure" („Stuttgarter Verfahren") has fallen out of use except for specific tax purposes, primarily in the sectors of property and inheritance-tax law. This method basically consists of determining the capitalized value of potential yield (productive or earning value) and the tangible value. The development of this procedure was heavily influenced by the post-W.W.II economic climate, which led to an over-emphasis of the tangible value or, in other words, of the value of the (undamaged) business enterprise just as it stood. The productive value of the enterprise, on the other hand, was figured solely on the basis of past results. On the whole, the Stuttgart Procedure, which ordinarily provides very low valuations of commercial enterprises, is now no longer an acceptable method of valuation for any purpose other than tax purposes; outside this sector it generally provides inaccurate results.

Due to the unsuitability of the Stuttgart Procedure, multifarious valuation procedures were developed that ostensibly took operational economic considerations better into account. The controversy over which method of valuation engendered by these so-called "practical procedures" was the best now seems at last to have come to an end in the Federal Republic of Germany. The most substantial contribution in this direction was provided by the publication of the opinion of the Institution of Certified Public Accountants in 1983 regarding the basic means of conducting a valuation of business enterprises. This led to the solid establishment of the premise that the productive value of a business enterprise is the sole relevant value. Of decisive importance, therefore, is the recognition that a business enterprise is worth only as much as the future withdrawable profits. In determining this productive value, the tangible value now has nothing more than a supportive function.

In the valuation procedure, the local statutory and tax law framework play an important role, and the purchaser or prospective purchaser should, therefore, turn the valuation over to a consultant who is well versed in these specific domestic regulations. Before entering into a valuation contract, however, the potential purchaser absolutely has to take the following points into consideration:

- The value of the commercial enterprise is always founded upon the individual perceptions of the prospective purchaser; it is impossible to appraise the value of a "business" as an object without clarification of such subjective value perceptions. Furthermore, the final price for the purchase of the business is not completely determined by rational factors. Prospective purchasers and their consultants or appraisers must, therefore, specifically define and determine the type of "business value" that is to be applied: purchasers could be interested in finding out the decisive value, which provides only the top or bottom price limits, and thus represents a neutral objective value that can be ascertained by using strictly non-subjective, verifiable value arguments or they could be primarily concerned with the determination of the so-called "fair settlement price," which consists of a compromise that also takes a certain number of the prospective purchaser's value perceptions into account. This function of the business valuation process should be made completely clear in order to prevent misinterpretation or misuse.

II. The Productive Value of the Business Enterprise

A. Problems and principles of appraising productive value

1) The value of a business enterprise is equal to the cash value of all its future net profits. In theory, that value is comprised only of the surplus earnings that can be permanently withdrawn without causing harm to the yield-bringing substance of the business organization. In actual practice, however, this pure theory has to be considerably modified.

For example, commercial law restricts the formal premises upon which a profit-distribution decision can be made and allows distribution only of those profits that have been judged to be in compliance with commercial-law regulations and on the basis of properly kept books. Due to such restrictions, a situation can arise where surplus profits do exist but, due to a lack of simultaneously distributable profits, are not available to investors. It is therefore essential to make additional assumptions concerning the future profit-distribution performance of the business.

2) When the distributable profit is used as a guideline, however, this immediately gives rise to the problem of the time placement of future yields. Such yields should be properly assigned to the periods of time for which they are anticipated. Of course, the further into the future the appraiser's projections are made, the less accurate they become. The appraiser should therefore weigh out the ascertained and projected yields for each future period of time in such a manner that their value on the key date will progressively diminish the further away from this key date the projections are made.

3) The same problem applies to the accuracy of predictions in general. Since the uncertainty of expected profit flow leads to various predictions, it is necessary to weigh each of the projections individually in terms of its overall probability.

4) The amount of future distributable profits for each of the future time phases of valuation must include a deduction of the accrued interest that could have accrued as of the key date, had the funds been invested differently. The internal interest rate (profitability) of an investment alternative is used to establish the rate of interest that ought to be deducted from all future yields. In other words, the future business profits are compared with the expected surpluses of an investment alternative. In determining this interest rate, the appraiser will ordinarily refer to the on-going domestic interest rate for long-term investments in the capital market. In the Federal Republic of Germany, it is common practice to use, as an orientation, the reports on investment returns on fixed, interest-bearing securities ("Umlaufrenditen") publicized by the Federal Reserve Bank of Germany ("Deutsche Bundesbank").

In some cases, depending on the purpose of the valuation (see the above delineation as to how careful the projected earnings are to be figured), it will be necessary to add a risk figure to the affixed interest rate. It is a matter of controversy whether the interest rate should be "inflation purified" as well. Normally, however, the inflation situation and inflation expectations have already influenced the capital market interest rate, and further inflation purification would therefore be superfluous. If the interest is "inflation purified", however, this should have occurred before any risk factor was added, since the result would otherwise include an "inflated risk."

5) The business enterprise must be valued in terms of its *total* function. This aspect is of particular importance to the mixed and affiliated enterprises frequently found in the Federal Republic of Germany ("GmbH & Co. KG," divided enterprises, joint-stock companies and silent partnerships), which are generally formed predominately for tax purposes. Experience has proven that it is extremely difficult to trace such divided enterprises back to a uniform object of appraisal. Furthermore, because such mixed businesses so frequently fail due to collisions with commercial or tax laws, statements concerning their valuation can be made only on a single-case basis.

6) The complaint is frequently made that the net worth of German enterprises is too low. If the total net worth is outside the currently common range, the appraiser should use empirical values (such as the common net worth of other enterprises within the same branch of business or the reasonable and proportionate amount of borrowed capital) to figure the total value of the corporation on the basis of normalized finance structures.

7) The possibilities of alteration to the enterprise which are open to the purchaser are generally not to be taken into consideration. Whether or not the valuation includes the future measures contained in the seller's plans depends on the purpose of the evaluation; in general, such proposals are taken into consideration only insofar as preparatory measures have already been initiated and implemented (e.g. the results of research and development projects or investments in equipment).

8) A past analysis should always provide the basis for appraising the future earning capacity but not, however, in the sense of determining a "yield sequence" that can be extrapolated into the future. Instead, the past results should be purified for extraordinary fluctuations or any infringements of accounting and valuation principles (including infringement of the principle of determining results properly according to time periods). Only then will it be possible for the appraiser to recognize the course of development and, proceeding on the basis of past development, to predict future turnover, draw up an investment plan, estimate the depreciation requirements and make a projection of the interest burden.

9) As already mentioned above, the tangible value of the enterprise is relevant only as the intermediate value of the business transformation process. In this regard, it simply represents previous expenditures and therefore has merely an auxiliary function in figuring the productive, or earning value of the business enterprise. As such, it is the essential object of reference in determining the amount of operating capital and the financial resources that will be required in the future in regard to all productive-value items that depend upon the tangible value. It is also indispensable as a foundation for investment planning (reinvestments!).

10) Personnel- related value factors (for example, the personal qualifications of the management staff) definitely play an important role for the purchaser. It is, however, questionable whether such factors should be included in a computed business appraisal since, in such a case, it isn't possible to arrive at anything more than very rough estimates. In the case of unincorporated firms or enterprises that are owned, operated and driven by individuals on the equity of their own names, however, it is both possible and necessary to affix a value to that equity and to do so irrespective of whether or not the investor plans to continue the business in its previous legal form.

B. Guidelines for determining productive value

1. Purification of past values:

The last three to five fiscal years should be considered and any nonessential operational assets should be eliminated. Expenditures and earnings should be assigned to the time periods in which they occurred. There will be some necessary modifications such as depreciation on the basis of repurchasing costs, purification of extraordinary influencing factors and the ensuing changes (especially any changes relating to interest and tax expenditures).

2. Analysis of earning capacity

Once the purified past results are available, a quantity framework should be made on the basis of them. If it is to be successfully used for future planning, it must include the following elements:

- Prediction of sales
- Investment plan and projection of write-off requirements (age structure of production equipment, any repurchasing costs)

- Calculation of financing needs and projection of interest burden (non-operational expenditures)
- Projection of results within the sector of essential operational assets
- Consideration of personnel factors
- Separate valuation of nonessential operational assets
- Prediction of tax expenditures: this requires a supplementary calculation for determining the expected tax advantages.

PART II.

SPECIALIZED LAWS IMPACTING THE FORMATION, ACQUISITION AND OPERATION OF A BUSINESS IN GERMANY

Chapter 4

TAXES APPLICABLE TO BUSINESS ENTERPRISES AND THEIR DISTRIBUTED PROFITS

Joachim Knapp

I. Overview of Tax Laws

There are various kinds of taxes in Germany. Many of these taxes are easy to calculate and administer, result in only small tax revenues and have relatively little impact on the economy. From the standpoint of foreign as well as domestic investors, the following taxes are the most important:

- Personal income tax *("Einkommenssteuer")*
- Corporate income tax *("Körperschaftssteuer")*
- Business tax *("Gewerbesteuer")*
- Value-added tax *("Umsatzsteuer")*
- Capital-yield tax *("Kapitalertragssteuer)*
- Real-estate tax *("Grundsteuer")*
- Wage tax *("Lohnsteuer")*

A. Personal income tax

All German residents are obliged to pay income tax on the profits derived from agriculture and forestry, trade, self-employment, business, rental and leasing activities, capital investments and other sources. The tax rate varies between 0% and an absolute maximum of currently 53%, depending on the amount of taxable income. In the large majority of cases, even in the case of top-income earners personal income tax rarely exceeds 40%.This tax is levied only by the federal authorities, which is to say that there is no state or local taxation of personal income.

Resident shareholders who receive distribution profits from corporations are granted tax credit that may be applied towards their personal tax liability and protects them against double taxation.

B. Corporate income tax

Generally, a resident corporation is subject to German corporate income tax with respect to its worldwide income unless a tax treaty exempts particular items of income from German taxation.

A company is a resident corporation in Germany if it maintains either its statutory seat or its principal place of business in Germany. Limited liability companies and stock companies are generally liable to pay corporate income tax, whereas a partnership is not itself subject to such tax.

Taxable income is calculated on the basis of the profits of the business operation. The corporate tax rate on profits which are not distributed to shareholders is 50%. The rate applied to distributed profits is 30%.

C. Business tax

All businesses operating in Germany, including liaison offices as well as permanent establishments of foreign companies, are subject to business taxation. In determining whether a business is "operating in Germany," the decisive factor is whether or not the company maintains a permanent business location in Germany.

Although business tax, like income tax, is a federal tax, it is administered by the municipalities, which apply a certain factor to the basic business tax rates set by federal statute. Profit is the most important but not the sole basis of business tax. Business tax is based on 5% of business profits and 0.2% of business capital, which are both multiplied by somewhere between 300% - 500% in order to achieve the exact tax rate.

D. Value- added tax

Value-added tax (VAT) is imposed on the supply of goods and services within Germany, the importation of goods into Germany, the withdrawal of goods for the entrepreneur's own use and the payment of constructive dividends. However, exemptions from VAT are provided for the following: the exportation of goods, the granting of loans, the assumption of liabilities and guarantees, the deposit of securities and similar banking transactions, the transfer of securities, bonds, shares in closely held corporations and partnerships and transactions covered by the real-estate transfer tax. VAT is levied at 15% of the net sales price. There is a reduced rate, however, on books, food, agricultural products and certain professional services.

Apart from a few specialized exceptions, value-added tax is not a tax on corporate income or profit but rather a tax on consumption. In other words, VAT is a tax on the ultimate consumer. Admittedly, a business that sells merchandise in a taxable transaction to another business has to charge the net sales price and the applicable VAT separately. However, the purchasing business may claim the tax charged to it as credit against the VAT it charges its own customers. Every month the business pays the tax bureau only the amount of VAT that remains after it has deducted the amount of VAT paid to its suppliers for purchased goods and services from the amount of VAT it has levied on sales. The result of this procedure is that the final consumer is the one who ends up paying the tax.

E. Capital-yield tax

Income from stock dividends, silent partnerships in a business and bonds is subject to capital-yield tax. Germany's tax code levies capital-yield tax on distributed corporate profits regardless of whether the dividend is paid to a domestic or foreign holder of stock or other equity interests.

The company which distributes the income has to withhold the tax in order to pass it on to the tax office, except, however, in the case of dividend payments to foreign investors from countries with which Germany has entered into an antidouble tax treaty. In such cases the bilateral treaty takes precedence over the national tax code. The tax treatment prescribed by such treaties varies. Sometimes capital- yield tax is not levied at all. At other times it is initially collected and subsequently refunded in full or in part after all tax documents have been submitted and evaluated. The rate itself varies between 25% and 35% but can be credited against domestic income tax.

F. Real-estate tax

Proprietors of land and buildings are subject to real-estate tax at a rate that varies between 0.6 % and 1% of the defined value. It is very important to note that the "defined value" amounts to only 10% of the current actual value, which makes real-estate property tax in Germany very low and provides a lucrative investment prospect to foreign investors, who generally pay much higher real-estate tax in their home countries. The tax is fixed at the beginning of each calendar year and paid to the municipality in which the property is located.

G. Wage tax

Wage tax is a special form of income tax which is withheld from the salaries of employees by the employer, who in turn pays the withholdings to the tax authorities. As will be discussed in greater detail below, the type of tax which is applicable in any particular case depends on which legal form has been chosen for the business enterprise.

II. Tax and Accounting Impacts upon Establishments of a New Business or Acquisition of an Existing Business

A. Corporations

1. Incorporation

A corporation (GmbH, AG, KGaA) achieves legal existence through a formal act of incorporation (see Chapter 1). Following incorporation and application to have itself entered into the commercial register, a corporation must draw up an opening fiscal balance sheet. Generally, the asset side of this balance sheet consists of cash or cash equivalents in the bank and the liability side consists of items representing shareholder equity. This opening fiscal balance sheet must be submitted to the responsible German Revenue Office ("Finanzamt") along with a filled-out standard questionnaire for tax-registration purposes. The questionnaire requires information as to the names and addresses of the shareholders, the sales and profits predicted for the first two fiscal years and the number of employees. The information pertaining to projected revenue and profits is particularly significant. The German Revenue Office uses these figures to determine whether, and if so in what amount, a prepayment of corporate income tax and business tax is required.

2. Acquisition

A corporation can be acquired in one of two ways:

- through the purchase of all the stocks or other equity interests of the corporation

  \- or -

- through the purchases of the individual business assets.

a) Purchase of corporate stocks or other equity interests

The purchase of all the stocks or equity interests of a corporation (i.e. a change in corporate ownership) has no impact on the on-going taxation of the corporation. The German Revenue Office must be advised of the purchase at the end of the business year in conjunction with the filing of the corporate tax return. For several years now in Germany, the purchase of stocks or other equity interests in a corporation has not been subject to taxation.

b) Acquisition of business assets

The purchase of the individual assets of the corporation, as opposed to its stocks or equity interests does, however, have an impact on the tax treatment of the corporation. The corporation must replace the value of each individual business asset reflected on the balance sheet with the part of the purchase price assigned to the asset and begin to depreciate the costs of the assets at these new values over their projected useful life. If good will of the corporation has specifically been purchased, then this must also be assigned a monetary value. According to commercial law, acquired good will can be depreciated over a period of five years. The tax laws, however, allow for a good will-depreciation period of fifteen years. In other words; according to the tax laws, only 1/15 of the good will costs can be deducted each year.

In addition, any claims and liabilities that might have been transferred in the sale, must also be assigned a monetary value.

In general, when a corporation is sold through the sale of its business assets, the tax situation of the seller-enterprise has no influence on the tax treatment of the buyer-enterprise. It is nevertheless advisable to check with the German Revenue Office to insure that the seller-enterprise has fulfilled all of its tax responsibilities, including particularly the timely and full payment of all tax liabilities. In accordance with the Tax Code, par. 75 AO ("Abgabenordnung"), anyone who purchases an enterprise in its entirety can be held liable for a certain limited time period for the enterprise's past taxes.

B. Partnerships

1. Establishment

The law regarding the establishment of partnerships was extensively discussed in Chapter 1.

A partnership(OHG) must also prepare an opening fiscal balance sheet at the time of its creation. A partnership whose sole activities are those of a small, or lessor, merchant or whose income is derived solely from investments is not considered to be engaging in merchant trade as it is defined by the Commercial Code (HGB) and are therefore exempt from this requirement.

Nevertheless, all partnerships, regardless of their income-earning activity, must register their formation with the German Revenue Office and, in doing so, fill out a form requesting information as to the number of employees of the business and its projected sales and profits for the first two fiscal years.

2. Acquisition

As in the case with corporations, there are two ways for investors to acquire ownership rights in a partnership: either through the purchase of partnership interest(s) or through the purchase of the individual assets of the business.

a) Purchase of partnership interests

If investors purchase partnership interests without becoming the sole owners of the business, there is no change in the current manner in which the partnership is being taxed. Such a sale does, however, affect the individual tax treatment of the selling partner and the buyer. If the price the buyer pays for a share of the partnership capital is higher than its book value, a supplementary fiscal balance sheet must be prepared for the buyer / new partner which includes this excess amount and adds it to the book value of the assets that have indeed increased in value over time (i.e. assets with silent reserves whose real values exceed the values reflected in the balance sheet). If a residual amount still remains, then this amount is treated as good will and identified as such in the supplementary fiscal balance sheet. The portion of the excess amount allocated to the silent reserves of the business assets is depreciated over the remaining life of the assets. The portion of the excess allocated to good will can also be depreciated, and in this case the depreciation period is not the fifteen-year period mentioned above; rather, according to the rulings of the Federal Finance Court ("Bundesfinanzhof"), the depreciation period lies somewhere between three and six years.

b) Acquisition of business assets

Should an investor decide to purchase the individual assets of a partnership, the tax and accounting regulations discussed above under point A. 2. (b) need to be considered.

III. Tax and Accounting Aspects of Selected On-going (Typically Recurring) Taxes

A. Overview

Every business enterprise must prepare a commercial balance sheet once a year at the end of its fiscal year, whose twelve-month period may or may not be identical with the calendar year. On the basis of this commercial balance sheet, a fiscal balance sheet is prepared, which contains the valuations of the business assets in light of specific tax regulations. The maxim exists in Germany that the commercial balance sheet is authoritative for the fiscal balance sheet. This means that as a rule, the values contained on both reports should be the same. Nevertheless, inconsistencies can arise between these two balance sheets due to the differences in allowable good will depreciation periods or in the methods of fixing the value of stocks or other equity interests. As discussed above, commercial law provides for a good will depreciation period of five years, whereas the tax laws provide for a fifteen-year period. In addition, different methods of fixing the value of stocks or other equity interests can result in inconsistent fiscal and commercial balance sheets. This is particularly true in the case of partnerships because, while partnership interests are valued under commercial law at the purchase price, in the fiscal balance sheet such interests are valued at their net worth ("Kapitalspiegelmethode").

Although the commercial balance sheet is authoritative for the fiscal balance sheet, there are times when the opposite can be true. When such occasions arise, the valuations on the fiscal balance sheet must be carried over to the commercial balance sheet. If the business has made use of special fiscal depreciation provisions (digressive depreciation, special depreciation for investments in the five new states of the Federal Republic of Germany, etc.), then the resulting value of the business assets must be carried over to the commercial balance sheet.

B. Tax treatment of corporations

The profit figured according to tax law and reflected in the fiscal balance sheet forms the authoritative basis for recurring taxes. Such recurring taxes include business tax and corporate income tax.

1. Business tax

In order to determine the business-tax burden, it is first necessary to make various adjustments to the profit shown in the fiscal balance sheet. It must be increased by an amount equal to one half of the interest paid on long-term or permanent debt. Long-term debt includes loans which are available on a long- term basis for the strengthening of the working or operating capital of the corporation; for example, loans which provide financing for long-term investment projects or the acquisition of business assets. Interest paid on short-credit, on the other hand (for example, credit given for the purpose of financing a specific good and which must be repaid upon reselling the good), is not subject to this requirement.

In addition, any rent costs must be added to the profit figure contained in the fiscal balance sheet profit, unless the landlord is considered to be engaged in the business of leasing.

The law requires that not only mandatory additions to the profit shown in the fiscal balance sheet, but various regulations provide for reductions as well. The most important of them prescribes the reduction of the profit figure by the portion of it attributable to the corporation's earnings through its shares or other equity holdings in other corporations or partnerships. The purpose of this provision is to ensure that profits are not subjected twice to the business taxation. For that reason it can be applied only when the portion of the profit deducted has already been taxed once before.

Businesses which are defined by law as engaging in merchant trade must pay business taxes ("Gewerbesteuer") in all communities where they have a base of operation. For example, retail-sales stores or other trade enterprises that has a legally defined connection to the community are subject to this tax. The on-going business-tax rate varies from community to community. Although there is a uniform standard in effect throughout Germany that determines what constitutes profit subject to business taxation, the individual communities possess the fiscal authority to set the actual rate of tax themselves. Currently the business-tax rate ranges from 15% to 25%.

2. Corporate income tax

The profit figure shown in the fiscal balance sheet is also used to determine the portion of a corporation's income that is subject to corporate-income tax. This profit figure must, however, be adjusted by the addition or partial addition of certain previously subtracted expenses. To be re-added in full are the amounts paid for general property tax, corporate income tax and solidarity tax. As mentioned in the introduction, solidarity tax is an income-tax surcharge levied in order to finance the reunification of Germany. Other previously subtracted expenditures, such as outlays for the Supervisory Board, entertainment and gifts are only partially re-added. The new bottom-line profit figure is subject to corporate income tax at the rate of 46% -- but only, however, if it is not distributed to the stockholders or other holders of equity interests.

3. Treatment of distributed profits (dividends)

The part of the profit or annual surplus (as determined in accordance with commercial law) which is distributed to holders of stock or other equity interests is subject to a 30% tax rate rather than the 46% rate mentioned above. If the corporation knows at the time when the fiscal balance sheet is in preparation whether and, if so, in what amount its surplus will be distributed, it is entitled to apply the 30% tax rate to all profits marked "to be distributed."

If, however, the corporation decides to distribute profits from a previous business year after having already prepared the fiscal balance sheet and filed the corporate income tax return for the year in question, the German Revenue Office will either reduce the corporation's future corporate income tax liability or refund the excess tax. Under normal profit conditions, the application of the lower 30% rate results in a smaller corporate income tax burden. There are, however, exceptional cases in which the 30% ruling can amount to an additional tax load. For instance, if the company has no income or any profit subject to corporate income tax or if it is carrying back tax losses yet still decides to distribute earnings to its investors, it must pay the 30% tax on those dividends, even though it has no profit and normally wouldn't have to pay any corporate income tax at all.

Prior to yield distribution, the corporation must withhold the capital-yield tax (which carries a rate of 25%) from the amount earmarked for distribution and forward this tax to its branch of the German Revenue Office. In addition, the corporation must prepare a tax affidavit regarding the capital-yield tax, the 30% corporate income tax and the net amount of the dividends to be distributed to the holders of stock or other equity interests after the 25% tax has been deducted. It is the gross receipts and not the net dividends, however, which form the authoritative basis of the investor's income and which are then subject either to personal income tax or, in the case of a corporate investor, to corporate income tax. Following the determination of the investor's personal tax burden, the 30% corporate income tax as well as the withheld and already paid capital-yield tax is allowed as a tax credit or viewed as a prepayment of the investor's tax liability. The result, depending on the tax situation of the particular investor, is either a personal tax refund or additional tax liability. The purpose of this method of taxation is to ensure that distributed profits are taxed only once and at the tax rate applicable to the recipient of them.

If the recipient of distributed profits is a non-resident business entity or non-resident natural person, then the tax treatment differs considerably from that outlined above. The corporation that distributes the surplus profits is treated the same. Profits earmarked for distribution are subject to a corporate income tax rate of 30% and a 25% capital-yield tax. Foreign investors, however, are not entitled to the 30% tax credit. Due to the applicable provisions of antidouble tax treaties and the interpretations of these provisions by the German Revenue Office, the 30% is treated as a tax levied against the distributing corporation and not the investor. The rules pertaining to the 25% capital-yield tax differ with the investors and their place of residence.

If an investor is itself an enterprise engaged in merchant trade and owns more than 10% of the stocks or other equity interests of the distributing corporation, according to most antidouble tax treaties, its holdings are generally entitled to special tax privileges. Upon application, investors can receive a full or partial refund of their withheld capital-yield tax. Some antidouble tax treaties even entitle investors to receive their share of the distributed profits without deduction of any capital-yield tax.

C. Tax treatment of partnerships

The profit figured according to tax laws and reflected on the fiscal balance sheet is also authoritative for the on-going taxation of a partnership and its partners. This figure forms the basis for the business tax imposed on the partnership as well as the personal or corporate income tax liability of the partners.

1. Business tax

The way in which the business tax of a partnership is figured is no different from the way a corporation is taxed (see B. 1. above).

2. Personal income tax / corporate income tax

In contrast to a corporation, a partnership is not itself subject to income taxes; rather, taxes on the profit generated by a partnership are viewed as the responsibility of the partners of the business. The German Revenue Office must be informed of the extent of the individual partners' tax liability. This requires that the partnership provide it with a declaration of the total profit or taxable income of the partnership and the portion of it that is allocated to each partner (Par. 179 f. AO). Upon receipt of the statement, the German Revenue Office will issue a notice which either confirms or alters the figures. The notice becomes the authoritative basis for determining the amount of taxable income each partner has received.

If the partner is an enterprise that is incorporated in Germany or a natural person who resides in Germany, then its share of the profit is subject to either corporate income tax or personal income tax, as the case may be. If the partner is a non-resident corporation or non-resident natural person, its share of profit is taxed according to the provisions of the applicable antidouble tax treaty; or, in the absence of such a treaty, then according to Par. 49 of the Income Tax Act ["Einkommenssteuergesetz" (EStG)].

The majority of antidouble tax treaties follow the model treaty of the OECD (Organization for Economic Cooperation and Development) and provide that income paid by a German partnership to non-resident partners is income derived from engaging in business in Germany and therefore subject to German taxes.

If no antidouble tax treaty exists between Germany and the country of the non-resident partner, then Germany is entitled to impose a tax on such income in accordance with Par. 49 EStG.

IV. Liquidation or Sale of the Business Enterprise

If a decision is made to close down a business enterprise, the following tax aspects need to be considered.

A. Sale

There are two ways in which the investment in Germany can be ended through a sale:

1) the individual assets of the business can be sold

- or -

2) the stock or other equity interests can be sold in their entirety.

The German tax code provides for the following tax treatment:

- If the decision is made to sell the individual business assets, their book values must be compared with the prices at which they will be sold in order to determine the tax impact. If the sales prices exceed the book-value, the differences constitute profit earnings, which must be declared as such. The law grants partnerships important and unique exceptions to this rule. When a partnership sells all of the business assets, it has the possibility of choosing a method known as a "Betriebsaufgabe" (which means "abandonment or closing down of the business"). The result of this choice is that the profit is not seen as subject to on-going taxes, but rather is eligible for special tax advantages or privileges. The tax advantages of a "Betriebsaufgabe" are:
    - that the profit from the sale is not subject to business taxes - and -
    - the profit distributed to those partners who are natural persons is subject to income tax at only 50% of each partner's average tax rate.

If, however, the profit from the sale of partnership assets is greater than thirty million German Marks, no tax relief is provided.

If the decision is made to discontinue the investment by selling the stock, partnership interests or other equities, investors are always entitled to the special tax advantage described above; provided, however, that the investor is a natural person.

Corporate investors, on the other hand, who realize a profit by selling a business (partnership or corporation) must always pay taxes on it at the normal corporate tax rate. German law offers no tax relief to a corporation upon the sale or closing down of its business.

Before the provisions discussed above can be applied to non-resident investors, it must be determined whether Germany has the authority to tax their profits. The issue, in the case of natural persons, is resolved as follows: if non-resident natural persons who own up to but not more than 25% of the stock or other equity interests of a German corporation sell their holdings, their sales profit is not subject to German taxes. If their corporate holdings are over 25% or if they are partners in a German partnership, according to most antidouble tax treaties, Germany has the right of taxation and exercises it as outlined above.

Whether Germany possesses taxing authority over the sales profits of non-resident corporate investors or not is determined as follows: If the holder of stock or other equity interests is a non-resident corporation whose holdings in a German corporation do not qualify as a "Schachtelbeteiligung", the right of taxation does not lie with Germany (a "Schachtelbeteiligung" is intercorporate participation or mutual stockholding). If a foreign corporation's holdings of stock or other equity interests do constitute a "Schachtelbeteiligung", then as a general rule, Germany is entitled to tax any sales profit. If, however, the non-resident corporation has ownership interest in a German partnership (not a corporation), any sales profit is viewed as income derived from engaging in business in Germany, which, according to the antidouble tax treaties, normally falls under Germany's taxation authority.

B. Liquidation

If owners of a German enterprise wish to terminate their investment in it, yet do not want to sell the business assets, stock or other equity interests in such a way that the business will remain intact, there is only one option: closure through liquidation. A liquidation of a partnership requires a simple partnership agreement to close the business, followed by the sale of its assets or division of them among the partners. A closing balance statement must be prepared at the point where the liquidation is complete. The profit reflected on this balance sheet receives differing tax treatment depending on the length of the liquidation process. If the time between the partnership agreement to close the business and the date on which the last remaining asset was sold or transferred into the possession of one of the partners is three months or less, the liquidation process is treated as a "Betriebsaufgabe" (abandonment or closing down of the business) and any profit achieved is granted special tax privileges. If the liquidation process lasts longer than three months, however, any profit achieved in the course of it is treated as on-going profit and subject to both business tax and personal (or corporate) income tax.

The liquidation of a corporation requires:

- a shareholder resolution to liquidate which meets specific form requirements

- the appointment of a liquidator
- application for the registration of the liquidation in the commercial register.

On the date formally fixed as the date on which the liquidation process began, a liquidation-opening balance sheet must be prepared and an operational tax return filed. During the liquidation period itself, it is not necessary for the corporation to prepare yearly fiscal balance sheets or to file annual tax returns. The German Revenue Office grants a three-year leeway for filing tax returns to companies in a state of liquidation, which is to say, it does not require the filing of such otherwise mandatory yearly tax returns for up to three years. This means that a liquidation period which does not exceed three years will, for tax purposes, be viewed as a single tax year. Provided all liquidation procedures can be wrapped up within three years, the liquidator(s) has to prepare no more than a closing balance statement and file the final tax return at the end of the liquidation. The end of the liquidation must be certified by a Notary and entered in the commercial register. Agreement must be obtained from the German Revenue Office before the corporation can be removed from the register.

Chapter 5

ASPECTS OF GERMAN LABOR LAW

Matthias Abrell

I. Labor Relations in General

A. Persons covered by German labor law

German labor law can be defined as the body of law regulating work performed by individuals in a dependent position. The phrase "individuals in a dependent position" typically refers to employees ("Angestellte") and workers ("Arbeiter"), and it typically excludes independent professionals (architects, lawyers, physicians, etc.), commercial entrepreneurs (independent merchants, distributors, commercial agents, etc.) and all persons registered in the commercial register as a representative of a business (managing directors, members of the supervisory board or management board, etc.).

The borderline is sometimes difficult to draw between dependent employees and workers on the one hand and self-employed contractors or free lancers on the other. A relatively large gray area exists which contains persons who, while not personally dependent on an employer the way employees and workers, nevertheless rely on just one or a few businesses to such an extent that their position and need for social protection is similar to that of a regular employee or worker. Depending on the circumstances of the particular case, courts may not treat such persons as independent but rather as employees or workers who are subject to labor law rather than the normal civil law.

An important category of employees defined specifically in the law are executive managers ("Leitende Angestellte," or, literally translated, "leading employees"). Because of their managerial and/or supervisory responsibilities, "Leitende Angestellte" are given special legal status in certain areas of labor law, and the law very explicitly defines who falls into this category [see Par.. 14 KSchG, "Kündigungsschutzgesetz" ("Termination Protection Act")]. For that reason the terminology "leading employees" will be used here. They form a separate employee group for purposes of the law pertaining to the rights of business-unit employees. Moreover, compared to regular employees, leading employees enjoy only limited protection under the termination laws.

B. Employment in a business unit as opposed to employment in an enterprise

Dependent work is usually performed in more or less complex organizations. German labor law classifies such organizations basically as a business unit or enterprise. A business unit may or may not (alone or together with other business units) constitute an enterprise. An enterprise is an organizational entity which pursues an economic or similar purpose and is served by one or more organizationally connected business units. The distinction between a business unit and an enterprise is of importance primarily because of their different treatment under the Termination Protection Act and the law pertaining to the organization and authority of employees in business units.

C. Sources and categories of German labor law

The sources of German labor law are both statutory and case law. In many areas, the case law far outweighs the statutory law in both volume and substance. Many provisions of the statutes would be difficult to understand without the appropriate backup provided by the numerous court decisions. Case law adds life to the very dry and often not very detailed written law.

Whether German or foreign labor law applies in a specific case is an issue resolved by German courts on the basis of German international labor law. German international labor law is essentially based upon two principles. First, in the absence of an express agreement between the parties, the courts apply the law of the country where the work is usually performed. Second, the parties may not, through a choice of law agreement, evade those compulsory legal requirements whose purpose is to provide protection to dependent employees and workers at the place of their normal work.

German labor law can be categorized into six basic areas: (1) individual labor law, (2) collective bargaining law, (3) law pertaining to the organization and authority of employees in business units, (4) laws pertaining to the participation of employees in management decisions, (5) employee and worker protection law (including social insurance) and (6) procedural and administrative rules. The following is a short overview of these six basic areas.

II. Individual Labor Law

A. Basis of individual labor law

The fundamental basis of individual labor law is contract law. In other words, individual labor law refers to a set of terms which are agreed to between the employer and employees [note: for simplicity purposes, the word "employee(s) will be used from now on to refers to both employee(s) and worker(s)] and which govern a relationship in which an employee performs work for an employer in return for remuneration.

In principle, the employer and employee are free to agree on the terms which will govern their relationship. This principle, however, has quite a few exceptions. The most important exception is the basic rule that the parties cannot evade any law which is either necessary in order to uphold public order or to ensure a minimum protection for employees. In addition, there are certain legal provisions which may be changed only through a collective bargaining agreement and not by an individual employment contract. Finally, individual employment contracts, as a rule, may not change business-unit agreements, or contracts between the employer and its works council ("Betriebsrat") concerning the working conditions of the employees of the business unit.

To the extent the parties do not provide an express provision in their oral or written employment agreement regarding a particular matter, their contract is governed not only by written law, collective bargaining agreements and business-unit agreements, but also by case law, the common practice of the business unit concerned and the directions of the employer(s) within the scope of their authority to direct work performance. Because the number of legal sources influencing the employment relationship is extensive and it is often difficult to determine which rules have precedence over others, an employment agreement is highly advisable.

B. Termination of employment

One of the many problem areas of individual labor law for the employer are the rules restricting its authority to terminate employment. In fact, the laws pertaining to employee termination is an area which involves most of the time and efforts of experts working in personnel departments, employers' associations, law firms, and labor courts.

The basic set of rules is laid down in the Termination Protection Act (KSchG). The law applies to all employees who have been employed for at least six months in a business unit with at least eleven permanent employees. It does not apply to persons registered with the commercial register as legal representatives of a business or to comparable representatives.

While leading employees are protected by the KSchG, the nature of their protection varies from that afforded regular employees. For example, if leading employees challenge their termination in a labor court proceeding, the judge, if a violation of their rights is found, must dissolve their employment contract and, even if the termination was illegal, is empowered only to require the employer to compensate them for their loss of employment. Moreover, unlike regular employees, leading employees are not entitled to the preliminary works council proceeding prior to termination.

The KSchG provides that the normal termination of an employee is invalid unless it is justified by: (1) reasons existing in the person, (2) reasons existing in the behavior of the employee or (3) urgent business requirements preventing continuation of employment of the employee. In addition, in business units in which a works council is required, a termination is invalid if the council opposes the termination for specific reasons. One such reason exists when the council believes the employee could have been transferred to another job within the same business unit or to one within another business unit owned by the employer.

Vast collections of precedent cases exist for each of the situations mentioned here. Within the category of termination for reasons concerning the personality of the employee, many decisions, for example, deal with the issue whether sickness justifies termination. In the category of termination for reason of an employee's behavior, a multitude of decisions deal with problems arising from alcohol consumption, poor work performance, insulting behavior on and off the job, smoking habits, political activities, criminal investigations, private telephone calls, and many other aspects of daily work life which cause concern to employers.

The KSchG allows terminations for reasons of urgent business requirements in all cases where a fair evaluation of the opposing interests leads to the conclusion that under the existing circumstances the employer cannot reasonably be expected to continue to employ the person in question in his or her present capacity or in any other job within one of the employer's business units. Urgent business reasons justifying an employee's termination may be external or internal. External reasons may include declining sales, decreased profitability due to increased competition, exhaustion of raw material and the like. Internal reasons may include a change in working methods, the closing down of a business unit or a part of one, modernization of a system or methods or substitution of human by automotive work.

If employees believe their termination violates the KSchG, they have the right to file an appeal with the local labor court within three weeks. The local labor court has the power to either: (1) deny the appeal (assuming it finds no violation of law), (2) deem the termination to be invalid (which obliges the employer to continue employment) or (3) terminate the employment contract itself and order the employer to pay damages to the employee to compensate for the loss of employment.

In many cases, the parties do not wait for a final decision of the court but reach an in-court settlement terminating the employment and prevailing compensation for the employee. As a rule of thumb, the compensation is between one half and one full month's remuneration for each year of service (up to twelve years of service). Such settlements are appealing because a considerable part of this compensation is free of taxes and social contributions and litigation in the labor courts usually takes many months. Moreover, elderly employees or employees who expect to find alternative employment within a short time often prefer such a settlement rather than the continuation of a relationship with the former employer.

Whereas the KSchG covers most employees in most business units, additional laws provide termination protection for specific categories of employees, including, among others, members or candidates for the works council, local, state or federal parliament members pregnant women and invalids.

In the case of a normal termination, both employers and employees must observe the termination notice periods stipulated by the law. The length of such periods depends on the length of employment and the age of the employee. According to a decision of the Federal Constitutional Court ("Bundesverfassungsgericht"), termination periods are identical for employees and workers; such periods range from one month in the case of employment of less than three months to twelve months in the case of an employee over a certain age who has worked for the employer for more than twelve years. In all cases, the effective date of the termination must be the end of the calendar month.

An extraordinary termination with immediate effect, or, in other words, a termination that does not respect the mandatory notice period, is allowed only when it has been prompted by certain serious causes, which must be of such a compelling nature that the employer cannot reasonably be expected to continue the employment for the otherwise applicable notice period. As a rule, such compelling causes are limited to situations in which employees have deliberately violated important provisions of their contracts or other applicable laws. Such causes might be, for instance, criminal offenses, repeated refusal to work, illegal competition or breach of secrecy.

Special legal requirements apply to mass dismissals, or cases in which an employer within one month terminates more than five of the employees in small business units, 10% of the total staff or more than twenty-five employees in medium-sized business units or thirty employees in large business units. Certain procedures have to be followed in order to minimize the burdens on employees associated with the dismissal.

Prior to the implementation of such mass dismissals, the president of the state labor office must be notified and provided with a copy of the comments of the works council if any exist. This notification triggers a one-month period, during which no terminations may be initiated. It may be extended up to two months by the labor office and/or the labor office may impose certain restrictions in favor of the employees.

C. Effect of a transfer of the business on employees

One of the laws which takes precedence over contractual terms to the contrary is Par. 613a of the German Civil Code. This provision applies when a business or part of a business is transferred by contract to a new owner. According to Par. 613a, all employment relationships existing between the workforce and the former employer are transferred without change to the new owner of the business. Thus, the existing workforce is deemed to have contracts with the new owner of the business as of the date on which the business was transferred. Par. 613a applies to all employees except those who have already retired or who are legal representatives of the business. Further, the law expressly prohibits any termination of an employment contract by the old or the new employer due to the transfer of the business. The only legitimate ground for a termination in conjunction with a business transfer is if, due to changes in the organization of the business, the available work has been reduced.

Finally, the duty of the new employer to respect existing employment relationships also means that applicable collective bargaining and/or business-unit agreements must be honored and cannot usually be changed for at least one year after the transfer unless the new employer is already bound by another collective bargaining or business-unit agreement.

D. Non-competition agreements

One final and, as a practical matter, very important example of how a mandatory law takes precedence over a private agreement to the contrary can be found in the area of agreements restricting competition. Basically, the law requires that employees not compete with their employers during the term of their employment. This duty is imposed on all employees regardless of whether the parties have reached an agreement including such a non-competition clause or not.

Because employees often gather vast experience during their employment, an employer may desire to contractually extend the agreement restricting competition to cover the period after the employment relationship has come to an end. Such extended non-competition agreements are restricted by various legal conditions, which vary somewhat depending on the category of employee.

Basically, these restrictions require that any non-competition agreement must be unambiguous and in writing. Further, its terms and scope must be justified by the interests of the employer. For example, such an agreement may not cover a product range not offered by the employer or encompass a geographical area not served by the employer. The employee is bound to the agreement only if it does not exceed a term of two years and the employer agrees to compensate the employee during that period of time with an amount equal to at least 50% of his or her average salary, figured over the entire duration of employment with the company.

The above requirements do not apply to mere secrecy obligations, or agreements in which the employee promises not to reveal any confidential business matters of the employer even after termination of employment. The problems which can arise in the case of secrecy agreements, however, include the way in which the term "business secret" is defined and to what extent a secrecy obligation can be extended to include information that is, in fact, not secret.

III. Collective Bargaining Agreements

Employees in almost all areas of production, processing, distribution, trade and service businesses in Germany are organized in various labor unions. These unions are characterized by an effective and centralized organization reaching from the local to the state to the federal level. Both the unions and corresponding employer associations are protected by constitutional law and empowered to represent their members in employment matters and to negotiate collective bargaining agreements.

At present, the most important German labor unions are the "Deutscher Gewerkschaftsbund," which is abbreviated "DGB" (German Association of Industrial Unions), "Deutsche Angestellten Gewerkschaft" (White-Collar Union), and the "Deutscher Beamtenbund" (Civil Servants' Union). Special unions exist for senior executives. Like the unions, the employer associations are also organized on a state and local level according to industry branch.

The vast functions of the labor unions and employer associations include the representation of their members' interests at the governmental level (for example, providing input in the legislative process at various state and federal levels) as well as at the workplace level. From the standpoint of their members, the most important function of the unions and employer associations is most likely the negotiation and conclusion of collective bargaining agreements, or agreements directly providing rights and obligations for the union's and employer association's members. The traditional terms covered by collective bargaining agreements pertain to work hours, safety and other features of the workplace, maintenance of worker-qualification standards, general working conditions, and, of course, the basis of calculations and amount of wages and salaries. Although both unions and employer associations are bound to respect the agreement during its term, it is also their function to apply pressure upon each other by well defined legal means (the most drastic of such means may include strikes by the employees or lay-offs by the employer) in order to safeguard their members' interests in negotiating new or successor contracts.

Collective bargaining agreements are generally binding only upon the parties to the contract (union and employer association) and their members (employees and employers). Upon application, the administrative authorities can extend the agreement's application to all employers and employees of the branch concerned. In addition, even if the administrative department does not extend the agreement's coverage, the agreement may be adopted by businesses that are not members of the employee association and whose employees are not members of the union.

IV. Employee Participation in Business-Unit and Management Issues

A. Establishment of a works council ("Betriebsrat")

The basis of the law pertaining to the organization and authority of employees in business units is the Employee Representation Act ["Betriebsverfassungsgesetz" (BetrVG)]. This law provides that a works council has to be elected upon the employees' request in all business units with at least five employees. The law further sets forth the functions and authority of the works council and the extent to which the employer must cooperate with it.

Where an enterprise consists of more than one business unit and/or more than one legal entity, each business unit is entitled to its own works council, each legal entity is entitled to an overall works council ("Gesamtbetriebsrat") and all the legal entities as a whole are entitled to a group works council. The number of members in each of these works councils depends on the number of employees in the business unit, legal entity or group of entities, respectively. Moreover, depending on the number of employees, certain members of the works council at any of these three levels, may become full-time active works council members and thus be relieved of their normal work for the company.

The Employee Representation Act contains detailed provisions on the required cooperation between the works council and the employer. In order to enable the works council to fulfill its functions, the employer must inform the council of certain decisions, listen to its comments, discuss relevant issues with it, accept and deal with complaints and generally cooperate in good faith. Where no agreement or decision is able to be reached in matters requiring the consent or agreement of the works council, a conciliation board consisting of an equal number of members will be appointed by the employer and the works council, and a neutral chairman will be called in. The conciliation board's decision is usually final and binding. Appeals of its decision to the labor courts are possible only in very rare cases.

B. Powers of the works council

On behalf of the employees, the works council handles social, personnel and economic matters. As pertains to social matters, the employer must cooperate with the council on a great number of issues including working hours, interim extensions or shortening of work time, when, where and how wages and salaries are to be paid, general vacation principles, methods of controlling behavior and performance, social facilities, business housing, remuneration-structure principles, premiums as well as employee-suggestion and incentive programs.

The works council has the right to participate in general personnel matters such as personnel planning, the drafting of standard employment contracts and questionnaires, the establishment of performance-evaluation criteria, etc. Further, the council has important influence in individual personnel matters such as hiring, relocations and, most importantly, terminations.

In matters such as those discussed above, the employer must inform the works council of any proposed action and give it time to consider and respond to the matter. The council is entitled to object to it on the basis of specified reasons. Such objections, however, may be overruled by the employer or by a conciliation board. For example, in the case of a proposed termination of an employee, the council must be informed of the proposed termination. If the council raises an objection based upon an alleged violation of specified rules (for example, non-compliance with guidelines for the election of employees, the possibility of retaining an employee in another position, the possibility of continuation of employment after retraining or further educating the employee, etc.), the termination may be found to be invalid.

While the Employee Representation Act does not restrict the decision- making authority of the employer in economic matters, it nevertheless requires that employees be kept informed of and, to a certain extent, be given the opportunity to provide input into the development and implementation of measures which negatively affect or lead to the termination of their employment. In order to fulfill this information duty, the employer must inform the council (or, in businesses with more than one hundred permanent employees, a special economic board) of important proposed measures.

In the case of proposed changes to the business such as the closing down or transferring of business units, relocations, mergers or basic changes in the organization, purpose and facilities of the business, the employer must also discuss the proposed changes with the council. Following the discussion, the employer is then required to reach a compromise on issues of disagreement and conflicting interests ("Interessenausgleich"). If the employees will suffer disadvantages from the planned change, the compromise agreement must include a specific social plan. It is this social plan which comprises the major cost factor in many proposed business changes and often leads the employer to abandon the change or implement an alternative change which does not disadvantage the employees.

C. Participation of employees in company management

Whereas the representation law governs the participation of employees in decisions affecting their daily jobs, other laws provide for employee participation in the overall management of the company. This area is governed by the Co-Determination Act ["Mitbestimmungsgesetz" (MitbestG)], which essentially provides that if a stock corporation, limited liability company or comparable company employs more than 2000 employees, then its supervisory board ("Aufsichtsrat") must contain employee representatives. In general, 50% of the board of such companies must be elected by the employees and 50% by the shareholders.

When, during the supervisory board's meetings, a vote results in a tie, the chairman of the board has two votes. The chairman is elected by a two- thirds-majority vote of the members of the supervisory board. If no such majority support for a particular candidate exists, the members of the board who were appointed by the shareholders have the right to elect the chairman.

V. Employee Protection Law

A. Protection against workplace hazards

In the narrow sense, the purpose of an employee protection law is to protect employees from the dangers of their work activity. This type of protection law takes the form of individual acts of parliament as well as guidelines issued by the administrative authorities in charge of providing social insurance due to occupational accidents ("Berufsgenossenschaften"). The number of such laws and guidelines protecting employees from technical dangers in daily work and requiring the employer to take specific steps to ensure compliance with them (for example by appointment of people specifically entrusted with supervisory functions) is very large. This area of law is influenced by EC regulations and other EC provisions which have been adopted on the basis of Art. 118 und 118a of the EC Treaty.

B. Mandatory social security

The broader definition of employee protection encompasses laws requiring mandatory social security. Social security is insurance which protects employees from the consequences of sickness, old age or other disabilities as well as from the loss of employment (unemployment insurance). At the current time social security payments amount to almost 20% of an employee's gross monthly salary. One half of the amount is deducted from the employee's personal paycheck; the other half is paid by the employer above and beyond the gross salary.

These mandatory social security payments are often viewed by employees as a "second income tax." Their high costs are one of the reasons that some people attempt to avoid being classified as employees and instead seek to work for a business as a self-employed contractor or in some other capacity which does not qualify as dependent labor.

VI. Labor Authorities and Courts

A. Administrative authorities

The Federal Department of Labor and Social Order ("Bundesministerium für Arbeit und Sozialordnung") is the top federal authority in the area of labor administration. It is responsible for the Federal Labor Court ("Bundesarbeitsgerichtshof"), the Federal Office of Labor Protection and Accident Research, the Federal Labor Office ("Bundesanstalt für Arbeit") and the Federal Institute for Professional Education.

The German federal states also have labor departments, which are concerned with labor policy, labor courts, wages and tariffs, settlement issues, and all other details of dependent labor. In addition, on the state level there are also numerous specialized authorities dealing with protecting the employee from the dangers associated with work. These authorities include the trade supervisory office ("Gewerbeaufsichtsamt"), the local mining authorities ("Bergamt") and the Head Office for Public Assistance

("Hauptfürsorgestelle"), which provides social protection to invalids.

The administration of work-related educational and unemployment programs and monetary payments to employed or unemployed persons is largely the task of the Federal Labor Office ("Bundesanstalt für Arbeit"). Its primary function is the administration of payments to the unemployed including people who have lost their jobs due to their employer's bankruptcy. The Federal Labor Office consists of its main office in Nuremberg, nine offices on the state level, and approximately one hundred and fifty local labor offices, not counting the local labor offices in the new German states, which are just now in the process of being established.

B. Labor courts

The German labor courts are organized on three levels. The first level is the local labor court which is responsible for handling all disputes arising in individual labor relationships (including collective bargaining law) or questions concerning the organization or authority of the employees in business units. While its procedure is governed by many of the same provisions applicable in the general civil court, there are nevertheless important differences. Decisions of the local labor court may be appealed to the state labor court and, in certain cases, to the Federal Labor Court.

One of the main drivers behind the three-tier system was the public desire to make judicial recourse in labor issues affordable by virtually everyone. At the local labor-court level, the losing party need not reimburse the winning party for its costs. In addition, in determining the litigation value, the court attempts to set the value as low as reasonably possible. The benefits to the party seeking justice are obvious since legal fees and court costs are set according to the litigation value.

Despite such rules and practices, however, employees (especially in termination cases) may be harmed by the long length of time that generally elapses between the filing of their action and the receipt of a court decision. This holds especially true in times of relatively high national unemployment. In such times, the work load of the labor courts increases substantially as almost every termination that the works council opposes is appealed to the courts.

Chapter 6

RESIDENCE AND WORK PERMITS

Michael Wendler

I. Law Applicable to Foreigners Who Wish to Reside (Temporarily or Permanently) in the Federal Republic of Germany

A. Residency issues

The most important source of the German laws pertaining to residency issues is the Aliens Act ["Ausländergesetz" (AuslG)]. This legal code addresses two types of residency: permanent and temporary. Throughout this chapter, the term "residency" will be used to refer alternately to permanent or temporary stays in Germany. Its exact meaning can be derived from the context.

1. Residency requires permission

The general rule is that foreigners who wish to reside in the Federal Republic of Germany (whether permanently or for the duration of a short visit) must receive official permission from the German government (Par. 3, sec. 3 AuslG). This permission normally has to be obtained in the form of a visa prior to entry. In addition, foreigners must be in possession of a valid passport in order to enter Germany and throughout the duration of their stay in the country (Par. 4, sec. 1 AuslG).

2. Treatment of citizens from the European Community

Citizens of the European Community are entitled to engage in self-employment or wage-earning employment to the same extent and under the same terms and conditions as German citizens. They are entitled to a residency permit and do not need a work permit.

B. Various forms of governmental permits which grant residency rights

Governmental approval of residency is officially granted in the form of one of several types of permits, each of which endows the foreign applicant with various types of rights and responsibilities.

1. Residence permit ("Aufenthaltserlaubnis")

A residence permit entitles foreigners to reside in Germany and is not linked to any specific purpose for residence (Par. 15 AuslG). It is initially granted for a limited period of time and must be regularly renewed (Par. 12, sec. 2 AuslG). Assuming all other requirements have been met, foreigners are generally not able to apply for an unrestricted residence permit, or permanent residence, until they have been in possession of a temporary residency permit for five years (Par. 24, sec. 1, no. 1 AuslG).

Typically, residence permits contain various obligations or conditions. For example, they can contain geographic limitations such as having their validity restricted to residence in one particular city, county or district (Par. 12, sec. 1 AuslG) or time restrictions such as having their validity limited to the time of employment with a particular business enterprise (Par. 14, sec. 1 AuslG). Further, the residency permit can prohibit all types of self-employment or any type of wage-earning employment (Par. 14, sec. 2, sentence 2 AuslG).

2. Residence entitlement ("Aufenthaltsberechtigung")

Under certain, rather strict, requirements, foreigners may be issued a residence entitlement, which endows them with much greater benefits than a residence permit does. One of the requirements necessary to obtain such an entitlement is that the foreigner must have been in possession of a residence permit for eight years (for foreigners married to German nationals, the time period is five years). The residence entitlement has no time, geographic or other restrictions and limiting conditions (Par. 27, sec. 1 AuslG). However, if the holders of such an entitlement leave the country for a period of more than six months, they automatically lose all their residency rights (Par. 44, sec. 1, no. 3 AuslG). Exceptions can be made if the local Aliens Office ("Ausländeramt") is informed in advance of such a planned extended absence from the country and the reasons for it. Holders of such entitlements can travel to or live anywhere in Germany. They have the same rights as the German citizen to pursue the occupational activity of their choice, which is limited only by the same industrial and trade laws and licensing or permit requirements that are applicable to all German citizens.

3. Residence grant ("Aufenthaltsbewilligung")

Residence grants are designed for instances in which foreigners wish to reside in Germany in order to accomplish a specific purpose. Such a grant generally authorizes them to reside in Germany until the specified purpose, which is set in a restricted time framework, is accomplished (Par. 28, sec. 1 AuslG). Such purposes can include: participation in training programs or attendance at a university, fulfillment of a particular function in a particular business enterprise or special joint-project endeavors.

Residence grants are valid for the length of time it takes for the bearers to accomplish their purposes. They can initially be issued for a residency of two years only. Extensions are possible for up to, but not exceeding, another two years when it can be shown that:

- the purpose has not yet been accomplished

  - and -
- it can be expected to be accomplished within a reasonable period of time (Par. 27, sec. 2 AuslG).

4. Authorized residence ("Aufenthaltsbefugnis")

If foreigners do not meet the requirements for a residence permit or if a ground for denial of a permit exists, they can still, under certain conditions, be granted authorized residence rights (Par. 30 AuslG). Grounds for denial of a residence permit might be, for instance, the applicant's pending deportation, lack of a means of self-support or reason to suspect his or her residency would impair or endanger national interests. Yet even in such cases, the applicants may be issued residence authorization papers if it can be demonstrated that their residence in Germany is justified by international law, compelling humanitarian grounds, or for the protection of the interests of the Federal Republic of Germany (Par. 7, sec. 2 AuslG).

5. Residence toleration ("Duldung")

Residence toleration occurs when the German government decides to officially tolerate the otherwise illegal residency of a foreigner. Such a permit is primarily granted to cover the period of time in which compelling legal or factual reasons make it impossible for the authorities to deport the alien, such as for instance, when he or she faces a danger of torture (Par. 53, sec. 1 AuslG) or the death penalty (Par. 53, sec. 2 AuslG) if returned to his or her country of origin. Residence-toleration papers can also be issued for other compelling humanitarian reasons based on international law or on similar grounds (Par. 53, sec. 3 AuslG).

C. Different purposes of residency

The type of permit foreigners are required to have depends on the purpose of their residency in Germany.

1. Temporary residence for non-occupational purposes with a permit

As a general rule foreigners who wish to temporarily reside in Germany for tourist, cultural, scientific, sport or other private, non-occupational, purposes are required to receive permission from the German government (Par. 3, sec. 3 AuslG). The type of permit granted for such purposes does not entitle the foreigner to engage in occupational activity while in the country.

Occupational activity is defined to include all self-employment or wage- earning employment which meets one of the following criteria:

- activity which is designed to lead to a profit,
- a type of activity which is typically remunerated

  - or -
- activity which per agreement is to be remunerated (Par. 12, sec. 1 of the regulations adopted pursuant to AuslG).

Despite this rather all-encompassing definition, the law provides for several clearly specified exceptions.

Employees of a foreign business enterprise are not considered to be "engaging in occupational activity" if they maintain residence in their country of origin, do not reside in Germany longer than three months and are:

- members of the part of the enterprise's work force which is involved in the transport of people or goods between countries [Par. 12, sec. 2, no. 2 "Duchführungsverordnung zum Ausländergesetz" (DVAuslG)];
- involved in setting up, assembling or servicing a machine which has been delivered by the foreign business (Par. 12, sec. 2, no. 3 DVAuslG)
- involved in meetings or negotiations on behalf of their employer or intend to enter into a contract (Par. 12, sec. 2, no. 1 DVAuslG).

The last exception cited above covers the situation in which foreigners enter the country temporarily in order to conduct negotiations or discussions pertaining to the founding of a business or other enterprise (through a lease or an acquisition contract) or pertaining to the establishment of a subsidiary company or branch office (through a shareholder or partnership agreement which has been approved and certified by a German Notary).

The above exceptions also apply to self-employed foreigners (Par. 12, sec. 4 DVAuslG), which makes it much easier for foreign entrepreneurs to achieve their business goals in Germany. They can use this three-month visa-free time period, for example, to prepare for the establishment of a business or other investment project, to pave the way for future business dealings or to actually enter into delivery contracts.

2. *Temporary residence for non-occupational purposes without a permit*

An important exception to the requirement that foreigners need a permit before entering the country (Par. 3, sec. 1 AuslG) is that citizens of countries on the so-called "favored list" (see attachment) are entitled to enter and remain in the country for up to three months without a visa.

While this permit-free residency exception does not allow the citizens from the favored countries to work in Germany, they are naturally entitled to engage in the occupational activity exceptions described in 1. above; for example, they can engage in negotiations for the establishment of a business in Germany without the necessity of obtaining any type of permit whatsoever.

3. *Single or repeated visits in order to engage in temporary occupational activity*

Anyone whose occupational activities extend beyond what is contained in the exceptions to occupational activity mentioned above and who does not intend to move his/her home to Germany must at least obtain a business visa. Such a visa allows foreigners to reside in the country for up to three months at a time and can also include permission for an unrestricted number of entries and exits during the course of a year, in which the time spent in the country adds up to a total of three months (Par. 28, sec. 4 AuslG). Extensions of up to three months are possible. With such a visa, foreign citizens are able to make business contacts and engage in the type of business activities which go beyond the discussion and negotiation exceptions discussed in 1. above. It should be mentioned as an important final note that international business people who must come to

Germany periodically to control the activities of a subsidiary company need no type of visa whatsoever.

4. Residence in order to engage in long-term occupational activity

With few exceptions (the largest one concerning citizens of the European Community), foreigners who wish to engage in self-employment or wage-earning employment in Germany and who either currently live in the country or plan to move here, must first be in possession of a permit which allows them to work and reside in Germany.

Normally, the government requires that foreigners be in possession of or be entitled to a residence permit or residence authorization (as mentioned above, the latter grants the right to residence in connection with a particular purpose) before they can obtain permission to engage in occupational activity.

D. Procedure and jurisdiction

It is possible to receive governmental permission to reside in Germany only if the foreigners initiate the process themselves by filing an application. For this reason, it is important to consider the application-processing lead-times and to know which German authorities have the power to process such applications.

1. Time of application

As a general rule, foreigners who are not citizens of the favored nations or whose activities extend beyond the exceptions to occupational activity described in C. 1. above or who wish to engage in such excepted activities longer than three months or who intend to permanently reside and work in Germany must obtain permission to reside in the form of a visa prior to entry into the country (Par. 3, sec. 3 AuslG).

Excepted from this general rule are, in addition to European Community citizens, citizens of countries party to the European Free Trade Agreement (EFTA), including the United States. Such citizens are entitled to apply for residence permission from inside Germany (Par. 9, sec. 1 DVAuslG).

Foreign holders of residence permits must make sure that any restrictions contained in them concerning self-employment or wage-earning activity that might be considered to be self-employment are removed before they engage in any occupational activity of this nature. This is particularly important in light of the penal provisions of Par. 92, sec. 1, no. 3 AuslG. Those foreigners, however, who are in possession of residence entitlements or residence permits which contains no restrictions normally have the same rights as German citizens to engage in self-employment or any wage-earning employment similar to self-employment.

Foreigners who are in possession of one of the other types of permits described above are rarely allowed to engage in self-employment or wage- earning employment of a similar nature. The employment office can, however, make exceptions to this rule upon the fulfillment of specific criteria.

2. Jurisdiction of the Aliens Office ("Ausländeramt")

The Aliens Office is primarily responsible for enforcement of the Alien Act (AuslG) as well as for resolving all other legal matters pertaining to alien residence and passports [with the exception of naturalization issues (Par. 63, sec. 1 AuslG)]. In any particular case, it is the Aliens Office located in the area where the foreign applicants reside or intend to reside which has jurisdiction over their matters. That means that applications for extensions and/or upgrading of permits (including the deletion or partial deletion of inconvenient stipulations) are, as a rule, be filed with and are determined by the local office of the Aliens Office, which has the power of immediate jurisdiction in routine matters.

3. Jurisdiction of German diplomatic representatives abroad

The Aliens Office does not have primary jurisdiction for the cases in which aliens are required to apply for permits and visa before entering Germany. For the handling of such cases, the Department of Foreign Affairs has empowered diplomatic representatives abroad (Par. 63, sec. 3 AuslG).

Such foreign diplomatic representatives working out of the offices located in the geographic areas abroad where the applicants customarily reside have general power to accept, process and in many cases make a decision on applications. For example, a Russian who lives in Vienna (as opposed to only temporarily staying in Vienna) must file his or her application with the authorized diplomatic representatives abroad serving the Vienna area and not the German embassy in Moscow. If the foreigner is applying for a stay of longer than three months or for permission to engage in occupational activity, the Alien Office located in the area of Germany where the foreigner intends to reside must agree to the granting of the permit (Par. 11, sec. 1 DVAuslG). The office located abroad nevertheless remains the office that actually issues the visa.

Foreigners who are from or have their usual residence in a country in which Germany does not maintain an office of diplomatic representatives must, according to Par. 10 DVAuslG, file their application for residence permission with the Bonn branch of the Aliens Office because Bonn is the home of the Department of Foreign Affairs ("Außenministerium").

II. Self-Employment and Other Occupational Activity Treated as Self-Employment

A. Types and conditions of self-employment

The foreigner who wishes to engage in self-employment or wage-earning employment which is treated as self-employment must be in possession of a permit allowing residency which neither

- contains conditions forbidding work

  - nor -

- is limited to such a narrow purpose that work by definition is excluded.

Wage-earning employment which is treated as self-employment includes positions in a business in which the employee has extensive authority to represent the company or can greatly influence management decisions in a manner similar to an actual business owner. One can distinguish between the types of occupational activity which are self-employment and those which are treated as self-employment in the following manner:

1. Self-employment in trade or business, as an entrepreneur or as a learned or artistic professional

Such self-employment includes:

1) activities associated with industry, trade or business such as, wholesale and retail sales, import/export, brokers, innkeepers

2) learned and artistic professionals such as painters, musicians, authors, journalists, engineers, architects
3) primary production enterprises such as agricultural or forestry enterprises

The following persons are also deemed to be self-employed because a partnership is not a legal entity and cannot function on its own:

1) A general partner in a limited partnership (KG)
2) A partner in a general partnership (OHG)
3) A partner in a civil-law partnership (GbR, or BGB company)

2. *Wage-earning employment which is treated as self-employment*

Although managing directors of companies with limited liability (GmbH) and members of the Board of Management of stock corporations (AG) are technically not self-employed, they nevertheless have extensive authority to represent the company. Without such persons, a company would be wholly unable to engage in business. For this reason, such corporate representatives are treated the same as self-employed persons. This is true even if a particular managing director has many characteristics in common with an employee. As is the case of self-employed persons, wage-earners holding positions that are treated the same as self-employment do not need a work permit [Par. 9, no. 1 AEVO ("Arbeitserlaubnisverordung")] in conjunction with Par. 5, sec. 1, no. 1 of the Employee Representation Act ["Betriebsverfassungsgesetz" (BetrVG)].

Persons involved in occupational activities which are treated as self-employment include certain agents whose extensive authority is prescribed by law (regardless of the form of the business) and leading management employees who possess general authority over company affairs. Such employees are likewise relieved of the duty of obtaining a general work permit (Par. 9, No. 1 AEVO).

In the process of registering a GmbH or AG in the commercial register, the local court typically checks to see whether any foreigner who has been appointed to represent the company and who customarily resides in Germany is in possession of a residence permit that allows self-employment.

3. Capital holdings in a business enterprise

Merely having an ownership interest in a business (for example as a silent partner or as a limited partner of a KG) is not generally interpreted as "engaging in occupational activity." This also applies to minority shareholders of a GmbH.

According to case law however, foreign owners can be considered to be self-employed if, for example, they own more than half of the holdings in the company and can exercise decisive influence through the voting process at shareholder meetings.

B. Requirements for foreigners who wish to become self-employed or engage in occupational activity treated as self-employment

Foreigners who wish to pursue self-employment in Germany and who do not qualify for one of the exceptions in I. D. 1. above, must obtain proper permission from the German diplomatic representatives abroad who are located in their land of origin <u>before</u> entry. Their application will be forwarded by the diplomatic representatives abroad to the Department of Foreign Affairs who will then forward it to the branch of the Aliens Office responsible for the geographic area which encompasses the intended place of residence (Par. 11, sec. 1, no. 2 DVAuslG).

Foreigners already legally residing in Germany but with a temporary residence permit whose conditions prohibit or limit self-employment or wage-earning employment treated as self-employment must apply in Germany to the local Aliens Office if they wish to become self-employed.

C. Input from other governmental or quasi-governmental authorities

The Aliens Office will often seek input from other business-oriented governmental offices and/or quasi-governmental trade organizations such as the Chamber of Industry and Commerce ["Industrie- und Handelskammer" (IHK)] before making a decision on a particular application of a foreigner to engage in self-employment.

Before giving their input, these other governmental agencies and quasi-governmental trade organizations consider such factors as the foreigner's citizenship, the length of time he or she has legally resided in Germany and whether or not the foreigner is married to a German citizen. They also examine the proposed form of self-employment in light of the following two factors:

1. "Important economic interests or special local needs"

The proposed self-employment is often considered to constitute "important economic interests" if it will

- involve considerable investment and /or the creation or safeguarding of an appreciable number of jobs,
- result in an enduring increase in sales or market share of other domestic enterprises

- or -

- involve the establishment of a manufacturing company whose product is technically valued (future demand is ensured) or particularly environmentally friendly.

2. "No harm to the economy as a whole"

This standard does not require a showing of a positive impact on the economy; rather, it is satisfied when there is no reason to fear that the planned form of self-employment will have a harmful effect on the economy. This standard is applied:

- pursuant to international agreements (for example, agreements with Australia, Finland, Canada, New Zealand, Norway, and USA),
- when the particular foreign applicant has legally resided in Germany for a long time (as a general rule eight years; however, five years for citizens of certain countries such as Japan, Turkey, and Indonesia)

  - or -
- when the foreigner is married to a German citizen and has lived at least two years in Germany and has been married at least one year.

If the authorities decide that granting particular foreigners permission to engage in self-employment poses a threat to the economy as a whole, their decision frequently has to do with certain personal characteristics of the applicants, for instance if there are past records of criminal misconduct, tax evasions or failure to make mandatory social security or other governmental payments. Another reason for denial on these grounds exists when the foreign applicants do not, according to German standards, have the requisite education and/or training to engage in the type of business they would like (for example, they have not passed the master craftsman's qualifying examination or the special examination for cargo hauling). The Aliens Office is not bound to accept the recommendations of other governmental or quasi-governmental offices though it generally does tend to act on them.

III. Wage-Earning Employment

A foreigner who wishes to work in a wage-earning, or dependent, position in Germany is subject to the provisions of the Aliens Act (AuslG) as discussed above as well as to a set of special laws pertaining to the promotion of employment ["Arbeitsförderungsgesetz" (AFG)]. The employment-promotion provisions serve, on the one hand, to encourage better integration of foreigners into German society and on the other to curb any further influx of foreign employees into the country on the other. Since 1973, a general ban on recruitment of foreign labor has been in place and allows exceptions only in certain very limited circumstances.

A. Permit requirements according to the "Employment Promotion Act"

With very few exceptions, foreigners who wish to work as wage-earning employees must first obtain a work permit from the Federal Employment Office (Par. 19, sec. 1 AFG). Employers are not allowed to offer work to anyone not in possession of a valid work permit (Par. 19, sec. 1 AFG). Such permits are issued by the local branch of the Federal Employment Office which, in the case of applications for general work permits, bases its decision on the current as well as predicted future conditions in the labor market and the circumstances of the individual case.

A general work permit often contains restrictions such as, for example, permission only to engage in a particular activity or to work only for a specific business enterprise (Par. 1, sec. 1 AEVO). It can, however, be granted without any restrictions whatsoever. A special work permit, on the other hand, is always issued without any time or other restrictions; moreover, it is issued without regard to the conditions in the labor market. Foreigners are entitled to special work permits if they have engaged in at least five years of self-employment in Germany during the last eight years (Par. 19, sec. 6 AFG in conjunction with Par. 2 AEVO) and additionally fulfill several other requirements. Foreigners who possess residency entitlements, however, regardless of their citizenship, are not required to obtain a work permit prior to engaging in wage-earning employment (par 9, no. 13 AEVO).

B. Exceptions to the regulations prohibiting recruitment of foreign labor

Despite the existence of recruitment prohibition regulations, it is possible under certain circumstances for foreigners to work as wage-earning employees in Germany. The legal basis for allowing such employment is set forth in the exceptions to recruitment prohibition contained in the Employment Permission Regulations (AEVO). These exceptions primarily include employment which is temporary by nature (such as employment connected to the foreigner's participation in general or continued educational programs or to a specific job- or task-oriented training program or employment as a professional athlete) and employment which is temporary according to law (such as a teaching or lecturing contract). Another exception allowing the granting of a work permit on a case-by- case basis exists if the Regional Employment Office and the highest regional branch of the Aliens Office agree that special public and economic interests support the employment of the foreigner (Par. 8 AEVO).

Despite the prohibition of foreign-labor recruitment, citizens of the following countries are given special favored treatment and may be granted a work permit without showing that any of the above exceptions exist (Par. 9 AEVO):

Andorra	Canada	Austria
Australia	Liechtenstein	San Marino
Finland	Malta	Sweden
Iceland	Monaco	Switzerland
Israel	New Zealand	USA
Japan	Norway	Cyprus

C. Employment through special work contracts

International agreements between Germany and a number of other countries often provide that a certain quota of foreign workers are entitled to limited work and residence permits for the purpose of employment on projects governed by special government-approved work contracts (for example, contracts for the building of houses and industrial construction work).

IV. Activities of Foreign Business Enterprises in Germany

A. Free trade

The business regulatory climate in Germany is strongly influenced by the generally very liberal provisions of the Trade Regulations ["Gewerbeordnung" GewO)], particularly by its principle of free trade. According to Par. 1, sec. 1 of the GewO, all people have the legal right to engage in business as long as they do not violate any necessary and lawful exceptions or restrictions that apply to everyone.

B. Business activities

Foreign business entities no longer require a special permit in order to operate in Germany. Rather, they are subject only to those permit and licensing requirements applicable to German businesses (for example, requirements pertaining to real-estate agents, loan / credit brokers, investment brokers, restaurants and hotels). Occasionally, Germany makes this equal treatment dependent on reciprocity and grants it to businesses owned by citizens of foreign countries whose government affords German businesses operating there the same courtesy. This reciprocity principle applies, for example, in the cargo-hauling industry.

Regardless, however, of whether a foreign business has opened a German office merely as an advertisement for the foreign business with no intent to do any actual business in Germany or as a dependent branch office (a business without its own bookkeeping system or bank account) or as a branch office which is registered in the commercial register, foreign citizens who live in Germany and work for such businesses as managing directors, board members or representatives with full powers of attorney must comply with the requirements described under II above.

Further, it should be noted that a foreign business entity will be viewed in Germany as a lawful entity only if

- it is so recognized in the country of its incorporation or establishment

  - and -
- when its administrative and business headquarters are located in the country of incorporation and establishment.

Proof of these facts can be provided, for example, in the form of balance sheets, affidavits of certified public accountants, leases and telephone bills.

C. Registration of business activities

According to Par. 14 of the Trade Regulations (GewO), the enterprise's business activity must be entered in the commercial register of the city or community where the business is located. In order to be registered the following documents must be provided:

1) An abstract of the business's foreign commercial registration translated in German or proof of the business's registration in a foreign register which is similar to a commercial register.
2) A document showing the authority of the person registering the business to act on the company's behalf in the event that the person's signature and representation authority is not established in the above abstract.
3) Proof of the location of the business through a lease or the affidavit of the landlord
4) Passport
5) A registration form, available in the business-registration office, must also be completed.

ATTACHMENT

Countries on the "Favored List"

Andorra

Argentina

Australia
as well as Coconut Island, Norfolk Island Christmas Island

Belgium

Benin

Bolivia

Brazil

Brunei

Burkina Faso

Chile

Costa Rica

Ivory Coast

Denmark

Ecuador

El Salvador

Finland

France
including French Guyana, French Polynesia Guadeloupe, Martinique, New Caledonia, Réunion, St. Pierre and Miquelon

Greece

Malawi

Malaysia

Malta

Mexico

Monaco

Nepal

New Zealand
including Cook Island, Niue, Todelau

Netherlands
including Dutch Antilles

Niger

Norway

Austria

Panama

Paraguay

Peru

Poland

Portugal
including Macao

Sweden

Guatemala	**Switzerland and Liechtenstein**
Honduras	**Singapore**
Ireland	**Slovakia**
Iceland	**Spain** including Spanish territory North Africa (with Ceuta Melilla)
Israel	**Togo**
Italy	**Czechi**
Jamaica	**Hungary**
Japan	**Uruguay**
Yugoslavia	**Venezuela**
Canada	**USA** including American Virgin Islands, American Samoa, Guam, Puerto Rico
Columbia	**United Kingdom of Great Britain and Northern Ireland** including Channel Islands and Island of Man
Korea (Republic of Korea)	**Cyprus**
Luxembourg	

Chapter 7

DISTRIBUTION AGREEMENTS

Michael Bihler

I. The Law Pertaining to Commercial Agents

A. Source of Laws

The primary source of German commercial agent law is contained in the Commercial Code (par, 84 -92c HGB). This law is nearly identical with the commercial agent law in effect in the other states of the European Community. The reason for this standardization is the 1986 enactment of a European Community directive (EC Directive of Dec. 18, 1986 ABlEG Dec. 12 1986 No. L328/17). This directive, which to a large extent was based on the German model, required the Member States to incorporate the commercial agent law contained in the directive into their own national law. All of the States of the European Community have now done so.

Most of the provisions contained in the HGB pertaining to commercial agents are mandatory; this means that such provisions are deemed to be binding on all principal-commercial agent relationships and any contractual terms to the contrary are void. In addition, even in those areas where the HGB does allow contractual deviations, another law entitled the "Law for the Regulation of Standard Business Terms" ["Gesetz zur Regelung des Rechts der Allgemeinen Geschäftsbedingungen" (AGBG)] allows such deviations only if the commercial agent is not unreasonably disadvantaged.

The AGBG applies to commercial agent contracts because as a rule such contracts are standard form contracts which have been drafted by a business enterprise for use by all its commercial agents. The AGBG serves to compensate for the relatively weaker bargaining position of a party faced with a standard form contract drafted by another through providing the party with certain legal protections. This is not to say, however, that no room exists for the tailoring of commercial agent contracts to the special needs of the parties. The following sections will discuss key aspects of the law pertaining to commercial agents and the extent to which deviations therefrom are allowed.

B. Commercial agent versus employee

A commercial agent is an independent contractor whose permanent business is either to act as an intermediary in bringing about direct legal relations between his principal and the third party or to enter into contracts with the third party on behalf of the principal (Par. 84, sec. 1, sentence 1 HGB). Whether a principal-commercial agent relationship has been created or whether the "agent" is in fact an employee is primarily a question of whether the "agent" possesses important distinguishing characteristics of independent activity. If this independence is not present, the commercial agent will be viewed as an employee (Par. 84, sec. 2 HGB).

Case law holds that the individual circumstances as a whole determine whether the requisite independence is present in any particular case. Criteria for such independence are that the commercial agent (1) is only to a limited extent subject to instructions and (2) bears personal business risk. These criteria are easily met, for example, when commercial agents are free to decide whether they will engage employees or contract workers and if so whom -- and if all of the agents' business costs are paid out of their earned commission. Additional indications that agents work independently include the existence of their own place of business and/or organization. On the other hand, contract terms which limit agents' choice of employees or impose such a strict reporting duty on the agents that an air-tight control system is maintained raise considerable doubt whether a principal-commercial agent relationship is present.

C. Contract obligations

1. Commercial agent

According to Par. 86, sec. 1 HGB, the primary obligation of the commercial agent is to act as a middleman in bringing about direct legal relations between the principal and third parties or to enter into contracts with third parties on behalf of the principal. This obligation must be fulfilled with the diligence of a "prudent businessperson."

A commercial agent also has a duty to review the financial soundness of new customers. Although not expressly stated in the law, this duty is implied from the HGB's general requirement that an agent represent the interests of the principal in his arranging and procuring of customers and/or contracts (Par. 86, sec. 1 HGB). If the agent failed to screen the economic background of new customers, a principal's interests could be placed in jeopardy. Agents have a duty to ascertain the financial soundness of a former customer, however, only if aware of a delay in payment or other circumstances which impact the customer's credit worthiness.

This duty to review the financial soundness of customers is satisfied by the agent's use of informal methods of inquiry. In fact, a provision in a standard form contract which requires commercial agents to procure credit information at their own costs is invalid. However, if, the agent is reimbursed for the costs incurred, the parties may stipulate in the commercial agent contract that official credit reports be obtained and/or credit research be conducted.

Another important duty imposed on the commercial agent is to provide the principal with all necessary information. This duty includes in particular the obligation to promptly inform the principal of all successful arrangements or procurements of business. The exact type of information the commercial agent must transmit is determined by the application of an objective standard. The duty to report should not be so extensive and detailed that it collides with the independence of the commercial agent. On the other hand, the parties may establish a reporting system.

Another duty which is implied from the law's requirement that the agent protect the interests of the principal, is the duty not to simultaneously work for the principal and for a third person who is involved in the same sphere or scope of business activity as the principal. The issue here is not whether the commercial agent's breach of this duty has actually caused the principal damage. Rather, activity which is in competition with the principal's business is prohibited because it disturbs the important relationship of trust which should exist between a commercial agent and a principal. While this duty flows from the law itself, generally a competition prohibition will be contractually agreed to by the parties in writing. In the event of a breach of the agent's duty not to work for a competitor, the principal has the right to terminate the commercial agent contract without prior notice. The principal may also seek contract penalties if they have been agreed to in the commercial agent contract ["Entscheidungen des Bundesgerichtshofs in Zivilsachen" (BGHZ 42, 59).

Sometimes the commercial agent may also be charged with duties which are atypical for commercial agent activities and which extend beyond what is normally expected of an agent. The imposition of such additional obligations (for example, the duty to stock goods) raises the issue whether the commission is adequate to compensate the agent for the extra duties or whether additional claims for remuneration exist.

2. Principal

Among other duties, the principal must provide the commercial agent with all that an agent reasonably needs from a principal in order to fulfill his responsibilities. This duty includes, in particular, the responsibility to keep the agent thoroughly informed (Par. 86a, sec. 2, sentence 1 HGB).

Principals remain free however, to independently manage their businesses and are therefore under no obligation to involve commercial agents in this process. Decisions regarding production, marketing and sales, quality and price of goods are exclusively the province of the principal.

The only limitation to the principal's exclusive management right is the arbitrariness prohibition. If the principal, for example, arbitrarily and without a valid reason, discontinues or suspends production, commercial agents must be advised in advance. If the principal fails to provide such advance notice, then the agents may be entitled to damages.

D. Commercial agents' commissions

1. General, regional and sole agents

According to Par. 87, sec. 1 HGB, the commercial agent is entitled to a commission on all contracts entered into during the time that a commercial agent contract is in effect and which are either (1) the result of the activity of the agent or (2) entered into with a third party who the agent had previously contacted regarding the same type of goods. Under this standard, the agent's activity need not be the sole or the primary cause of the contract between the principal (or the dealer on the principal's behalf) and customer. It is sufficient if the agent's actions are only one of the reasons for such contract. In addition, the agent is entitled to a commission on all reorders or subsequent contracts unless the commercial agent contract specifically and expressly provides otherwise.

Often a type of commercial agent, known as a regional agent, will be assigned a specific area and/or circle of customers. In this case, the agent is not only entitled to a commission on contracts he or she has helped to secure but rather on all contracts with customers from this geographic area or customer circle which are entered into during the time that the commercial agent contract is in effect. In addition, regional agents can require that the principal ensure that their territory is respected by other agents.

Another common type of commercial agent is the "sole" agent ("exclusive agent"), who, as the name suggests, possesses the sole right to represent the principal in an assigned geographic area. Like the regional agent, the sole agent is entitled to a commission on all contracts with customers from his or her assigned territory. Unlike regional agents, however, sole agents enjoy the additional right that even the sales and marketing activity of the principal in the agents designated territories is excluded unless the commercial agent contract specifically provides otherwise.

2. Overhang commission

Under the law, the commercial agent is entitled to a commission on sales which occur after the expiration or termination of the commercial agent contract if the agent has arranged or procured the sale or taken such preparatory steps that the sale can be said to be primarily the result of the agent's activities; or, if before the agent-principal relationship came to an end, the principal had received an offer to buy from a third person (Par. 87, sec. 3 HGB).

This right of agents to a payment of commission on sales occurring after the expiration of their commercial agent contract ("overhang commission") can however, be contractually modified or eliminated if a factually justifiable reason for it exists. According to a precedent case ruling, a justifiable reason exists if, at the beginning of the contract term, the commercial agent receives commissions on sales that his or her predecessor initiated and the agent's successor likewise receives the commissions on any sales occurring after the agent's contract expires.

3. Unilateral changes to contract terms

As a rule, contract provisions which allow the principal to make unilateral changes during the duration of the commercial agent contract such as, for example, unilaterally altering the agent's rate of commission, the borders of the assigned geographical area or the products which said agent handles on behalf of the principal are unenforceable. The only options for a principal who wishes to make a unilateral change are: (1) in the case of a commercial agent contract with an unspecified duration, to make use of a special type of termination known as a "Änderungskündigung," which is a termination of the contract with the simultaneous option of renewal under altered conditions or (2) to connect the reservation of right to make unilateral changes to a specific reasonable set of circumstances; such as for example, the reduction of the assigned geographical area if sales are reduced.

4. Manifestation of the agent's right to a commission

Under Par. 87a HGB, the commercial agent has a right to a commission at the time the sales transaction is carried out. This means that the agent's entitlement occurs as soon as the principal has delivered the goods, regardless of whether or not the customer has paid for them. The parties can, however, contractually deviate or modify this rule (Par. 87a, sec. 1 HGB). One typical modification is for the parties to agree that the agent is not entitled to a commission until the third person has acted on the sales contract; that is, until the customer has actually made payment. This particular modification, which is generally regarded as enforceable, results in the commercial agent bearing the full risk for the execution of the contract.

5. Miscellaneous mandatory rights impacting agent's commission

If commercial agents agree to guarantee the payment of the procured customers ("del credere agent"), then they are entitled to an additional commission (Par. 86b HGB). Another mandatory provision regarding the commission is contained in Par. 87a, sec. 3 HGB. According to this provision, commercial agents are entitled to a full commission on any contract they have entered into with the customer even if the contract terms are subsequently partly or completely not fulfilled; provided, however, that the partial or total lack of fulfillment are due to circumstances for which the principal is responsible.

Par. 87 of the HGB ensures that commercial agents are remunerated for their efforts when, based on reasons that have to do with the relationship between the principal and the third party, the contract is not executed. Contract terms which attempt to deviate from this law, for example, a stipulation that the agent is not entitled to a commission in the event the principal would suffer a loss if the contract was executed, or a clause which requires the agent to bear the costs in the event of a legal dispute with the third party are unenforceable.

On the other hand, agents are not entitled to a commission if the contract is not carried out due to reasons for which the principal is not responsible. Such a situation may arise for example, if a customer's default in payment results in the principal being legally entitled to refuse performance.

If the principal has reserved the right of "Selbstbelieferung," then the customer has the right to demand delivery of the goods contracted for only if the principal is able to acquire them. While such a reservation excuses the principal's performance vis à vis the customer, the agent nevertheless remains entitled to a full commission on the contract despite the principal's inability to perform. Because the agent has a right to rely on the principal's ability to deliver the goods which the agent has marketed in good faith, the fact that a supplier fails to provide the goods to the principal is deemed to be a circumstance for which the principal is responsible.

6. Amount of commission

The amount of the commission is usually agreed to by the parties in their commercial agent contract. In the event, that the contract fails to address this issue, however, the customary rate must be paid (Par. 87, sec. b 1 HGB).

Ancillary costs for freight, packaging, duties and taxes which the principal incurs and separately lists in the customer's invoice are not considered a part of the customer's payment for the goods themselves and therefore have no influence on the amount of the agent's commission. On the other hand, ancillary costs which are passed on to the customer but not separately listed in the invoice are considered a part of the contract price, upon which the agent's commission is based.

One exception to these general rules regarding the impact of ancillary costs on the commission is value-added tax. Even though VAT is separately identified in the invoice, it is deemed a part of the customer's payment for the goods and thus influences the amount of the agent's commission (Par. 87b, sec. 2 HGB). However, the parties may (and usually do) contractually deviate from this law and instead agree not to consider the amount of value-added tax in determining the agent's commission.

A discount or other type of price reduction granted the customer has no impact on the amount of the commission. A provision in the commercial agent contract to the contrary is unenforceable. And, finally, even if the parties agree to a reduction in the commission in the event the principal helps the agent to secure a contract, a Federal Court ruling holds that such an agreement is likewise of no force and effect.

The agent's commission must be calculated and paid on a monthly basis; however, the parties may agree instead to a three-month payment period. The actual payment to the agent must be made no later than the end of the month which follows the relevant accounting period (Par. 87c, sec. 1 HGB).

Agents have a right to all information contained in the principal's books or ledgers which are relevant to the calculation of their commission; for example, the names and addresses of all customers who placed an order, the type, amount and price of the sold goods, and information pertaining to returns and failures to carry through with transactions (but not, however, the reason for such returns or failures). Providing the agent with copies of customers' invoices alone is not sufficient. Because the agent's right to information is only extinguished when both parties are in agreement regarding the commission, it is recommended that the principal collect the necessary information at the time the agent's commission is calculated and then send such information to the agent along with the commission payment.

These laws regarding the settlement of the commercial agent's account are obligatory, and any agreement by the parties which limits the agent's legal protections in this regard are unenforceable. Monetary claims of either party arising out of the principle-agent relationship are subject to a four-year statute of limitations. The period begins to run with the end of the year in which the claim becomes due. It is usually not possible for the parties to bind themselves to a shorter limitations period; and at least in an AGB ("Allgemeine Geschäftsbedingungen") contract, a standard form commercial agent contract subject to the Law for the

Regulation of Standard Business Terms, this is true even if the shortened limitation period applies to both parties.

E. Termination of the commercial agent contract

A commercial agent contract with an unspecified duration or term may be terminated without cause by a one-month advance notice in the first year of the contract, a two-month advance notice in the second year, a three-month advance notice in the third to fifth year and a six-month advance notice after the fifth year. The termination's effective date is the last day of the calendar month, unless the parties have provided otherwise in their contract (Par. 89, sec. 1 HGB). The length of the notice period can be extended by contract but not shortened. Even if the commercial contract provides for a probationary period, the above stated notice periods must be provided.

The Federal Court has ruled that it is not possible to terminate only a part of the commercial agent contract unless the parties have agreed otherwise and such termination is limited to a part of the agent's activity that is capable of being separated from his or her other activities. A termination of the commercial agent contract for an important reason (due cause) can be immediately effected by either party without the necessity of providing advance notice (Par. 89a HGB). This termination right can neither be excluded nor limited by contract.

Important reasons for termination are facts which result in it being unreasonable to expect a party to keep the contract in force until the advance notice period has expired. Agreements in advance regarding which specific types of factual situations constitute important reasons are somewhat problematical. Basically, an important reason is a situation or set of facts which have resulted in a shock to the relationship of trust between the principal and agent. For example, important reasons for the agent to terminate without notice could be an arbitrary, significant reduction of the commission rate by the principal or exploitation of the agent's efforts by a firm in which the principal has an ownership interest. Important reasons for the principal to terminate without notice could be, for example, the agent's definitive, unauthorized refusal to work, an agent's attempt to entice the principal's other commercial agents away from the principal in order to advantage a third party, or placing fictitious customer orders. In addition, acts by the agent which involve breaches of trust are particularly susceptible of forming an important reason for termination. Insulting, libeling or slandering the principal; criminal activity; intoxication on the job as well as the failure to notify the principal of transactions or of certain facts which could be of particular importance to a principal, are examples of acts which can form the basis for a termination of the agent without notice.

If an important reason for a termination exists, then the termination must take place within a "reasonable" amount of time. Although the two-week time limit set by Par. 626 of the BGB is not applicable to commercial agent law, it is advisable, in order to avoid legal difficulties later, for the party in possession of an important reason to terminate to act on it within two weeks of becoming aware of it.

A party who terminates the commercial agent contract without notice, although it would <u>not</u> have been unreasonable for such party to keep the contract in force until the expiration of the notice period, may be liable to the other party for damages. For this reason, a commercial agent contract should not be terminated without notice until the justification thereto has been carefully examined. The trend in the case law is to view the types of termination reasons which render it unreasonable to keep the contract in force until the advance notice period has expired, as quite limited.

Finally, if the principal wishes to implement a termination without notice based on a reason which concerns the agent's performance (as opposed, for example, to conduct which involves a breach of trust), then prior to the termination, the agent is first entitled to a warning. This warning must be in writing and describe the conduct which the principal finds contrary to their agreement as well as contain a statement that in the event such conduct is continued, the contract will be terminated.

F. Compensatory claim of agent for loss of clientele

A commercial agent's work results in the development of a regular group of customers or clientele. This valuable service to the principal is not only remunerated through commissions, but also through a payment at the time of the termination of the commercial agent contract which compensates the agent for his loss of clientele (Par. 89b HGB). Because the amount of this compensatory payment very often leads to a disagreement between the parties at the time the contract is terminated, it will be discussed here in detail.

First of all, this compensatory claim is not required upon the termination of all commercial agent contracts. According to Par. 89b, sec. 3 HGB, the payment is not required when it is the agent who terminates the contract unless said termination is justified by an important reason for which the principal is responsible. It is important to note that when the age of agents is the reason for termination, they are always entitled to a compensatory payment.

Likewise, if the principal justifiably terminates the contract based on important reasons for which the agent is responsible, the agent's compensatory right is forfeited.

Terminations where no compensatory payment is required, are the exception. Usually, when a commercial agent contract is terminated, it is a termination initiated by the principal with notice and without the existence of an important reason which would justify a termination without notice. In such a typical termination, agents are entitled to a compensatory payment upon request if: (1) during the contract term they have made contacts with new customers and (2) such contacts could lead to considerable advantage for the principal following termination of the principal-agent relationship (Par. 89b, sec. 1 HGB).

The first requirement listed above (contact with new customers) is also deemed to be met if, as a result of the agent's activities, the business relationship with a former customer who had not been originally secured by the agent, is significantly intensified. Generally, a significant intensification of a business relationship can be shown if, during the duration of the commercial agent contract, the sales figures corresponding to such previously secured customer are doubled.

If the principal demands that a new agent pay an "admission fee" for the right of assuming representation of the existing customers of an agent who is leaving, then this fee has no impact on the question whether said departing agent was the one who had initially contacted and/or intensified relations with these customers. Also the new agent is not entitled, in the event his or her contract is subsequently terminated, to have the amount of the "admission fee" returned in the form of a compensatory payment. It is, however, possible for the parties to specifically agree that upon termination, the agent is entitled to a minimum compensatory payment equal to the amount originally paid by the agent as an "admission fee." Such an agreement is sometimes included in the parties' contract in order to protect the agent who has paid an admission fee from an unexpected early termination of the commercial agent contract.

The second requirement listed above (provision of considerable advantage to the principal) is met upon a showing that as a result of the termination of the commercial agent contract, the agent will lose commissions on existing or future contracts with new customers originally secured by the agent and/or with former customers whose business relations with the principal the agent has been successful in significantly increasing. The amount of the agent's loss of commissions is generally equivalent to the advantage the principal would enjoy if no compensatory payment was required. Therefore, a forecast of how the business relationships between the principal and such customers will develop in the future and how much commission the agent would have earned if the contract with the agent had not been terminated must be made. The question whether and to what extent changes in the established clientele can be expected are particularly important in making this forecast.

The determination of the amount of this compensatory payment must also take into account all circumstances which bear on the fairness of the payment. In this connection, the reasons why the commercial agent contract was terminated, the agent's family situation and support obligations as well as the question to what extent the product has developed a strong market appeal due to the principal's advertising outlays should be considered.

The first step in calculating the amount of the agent's compensatory payment is to determine the agent's total annual commissions earned in the last year of the principal-agent relationship on contracts with new customers or with existing customers whose business relations with the principal the agent succeeded in considerably intensifying. The second step is to determine how many years in the future the principal can expect to do business with this particular customer pool. It is generally assumed that such relationships will continue for two to five years beyond the termination date of the commercial agent contract. The number of years or forecast period chosen depends on and corresponds to the overall rate of customer fluctuation one can expect in the particular situation. For example, if the parties choose a four-year period, this means that they assume that the principal will annually lose 25% of the new or intensified customer relationships which are attributable to the agent's efforts.

The third step is to take the figure derived from step one and project it over the forecast period in order to determine the agent's gross compensatory payment. The sum determined in this way represents the gross compensatory payment. The fourth step is to reduce this gross sum by the amount of interest advantage which will accrue to the agent due to receiving future commissions on a lump-sum basis. The fifth step is to consider if further reductions should be made based on reasons of fairness and, if so, to make such reductions.

Finally, the sum which results from the fifth step must be compared to the highest amount of compensatory payment allowed by law. This comparison is necessary because according to Par. 89b, sec. 2 HGB, the compensatory payment may not exceed the average yearly commissions or other income earned by the agent in the last five years.

The laws pertaining to this compensatory payment are mandatory; in particular, any attempt by the parties to avoid the compensatory payment or provide for a reduced payment *ahead of time* are strictly without legal effect. The only way that the parties may contractually impact this compensatory payment is through an agreement entered into after the commercial agent relationship has been terminated.

In such a post termination agreement, it is customary for the agent and principal to determine the amount of the compensatory payment. The parties may also extinguish the agent's right to a compensatory payment altogether if they agree that a third person shall take the place of the former commercial agent and this substitution actually occurs. Again, it is important to emphasize that such agreements are only possible after the commercial agent contract has been terminated.

Commercial agents must assert their claims to compensatory payments within one year following termination of the commercial agent contract or they lose them. It is also possible for the agent to assert his claim prior to the termination of the contract. The law neither prescribes a particular form for the assertion of this right, nor requires that it be asserted through the courts.

G. Non-competition agreements

The principal and agent may legally enter into an agreement that the latter shall be restricted in his or her business activities for up to but not exceeding two years from the termination of the commercial agent contract. Any such restriction on competition must be limited to the territory or the clientele of the agent as well as to the product or other matter that was regularly sold on behalf of the principal.

If a competition agreement is reached, however, the principal is required to pay the agent a reasonable compensation which corresponds to the length of time the agent's activities are restricted (Par. 90, sec. 1 HGB). This compensation serves the purpose of ensuring that the agent is provided with the necessities of life during the time the restriction is in place and represents consideration for the agent's promise not to compete.

The law does not address the amount of compensation the principal must pay. A reasonable amount is determined by considering the disadvantages that the agent incurs through the competition restriction and as well as the corresponding advantages for the principal. Other earnings of the agent are not deducted from the compensation; the fact that the agent has other earnings, however, is considered in determining whether the compensation is reasonable.

Up until the time when the commercial agent contract expires or is terminated, the principal may give written notice relinquishing his right to a non-competition agreement. Six months following the written notice, the principal is relieved of the duty to pay. Further, the agent forfeits his right to compensation if the principal terminates the contract with or without notice based on important reasons for which the agent is responsible. To ensure that the agent complies with a non-competition agreement, it is possible for the parties to agree to the imposition of contractual penalties.

H. International commercial agent law

If the principal's main place of business is in a foreign country and the agent represents the principal in Germany, the parties may contractually determine which country's law will apply. According to the Introductory Act to the Civil Code ("Einführungsgesetz zum BGB"), however, their contract may not violate the fundamental principles of German law designed to protect the rights of employees (Par. 30 EGBGB). This provision is applicable to commercial agent contracts despite the clear recognition under German law that commercial agents are independent contractors and not employees.

If this conflict-of-law issue has not been resolved by the parties in their agreement, the law of the place which has the most significant relationship to the contractual relationship applies. Generally, this question is resolved in favor of the main place of business of the agent and not of the principal (BGHZ 53, 332). This issue is nevertheless subject to debate.

In situations in which agents, regardless of where they actually reside, operate outside of the European Community, the parties may include terms in their contract which are contrary to all of the requirements of the German commercial agent law. In other words, the mandatory provisions of German commercial agent law (including Par. 30 EGBGB) are not applicable. The parties are free to agree to subject their agreement and the resolutions of disputes arising from it to the law of a foreign, non-European country.

II. The Law Pertaining to Authorized Distributors

Authorized distributors are individuals or entities who, on the basis of a long-term business relationship, buy and resell goods in their own name and on their own account. Because of the existence of a long-term contract between authorized distributors and manufacturers (or importers), the former acquire duties which result in their position resembling that of commercial agents. In many particular respects, the interests of authorized distributors and commercial agents are frequently similar. The courts have taken this similarity between the two types of independent contractors into account and in certain cases applied the laws pertaining to commercial agents to authorized distributors.

In particular, the case law holds that according to Par. 89b HGB, authorized distributors are entitled to compensatory payments for the loss of clientele at the termination of the manufacturer-distributor relationship if the following two requirements are met:

- the legal relationship between the authorized distributor and the manufacturer is more than a mere buyer-seller relationship. This is, for instance the case, when authorized distributors have become so integrated in the marketing organization of the manufacturers that their rights and duties resemble those of commercial agents

  - and -

- the authorized distributors are required to turn their customers over to the manufacturers at the time the distributor-manufacturer relationship comes to an end and the manufacturers are immediately able to make use of the customer accounts to their own business advantage should they so desire.

The contract between the parties is the starting point for determining whether authorized distributors are integrated in the marketing organization of the manufacturers. If authorized distributors are made responsible for certain marketing areas and if they are ascribed certain duties such as sales promotion or fostering the good reputation of the brand, this sufficiently indicates that an integration has occurred. The same also applies if authorized distributors are required to pay advertising costs, maintain a stock or are induced to sell products at the manufacturer's or importer's recommended price. Moreover, in each case, a careful examination should be made to determine if the actual day-to-day dealings of the parties deviate from their contract and whether the actual practices have, in effect, supplemented or altered the formal contract.

According to case law, it is quite easy for authorized distributors to prove that they are contractually bound to turn over their customers upon termination of their contracts. It is enough, for example, to show that they regularly turned their customer addresses over to the manufacturer during the time the contract was in effect, even if the manufacturer did not insist on insist on being given the addresses or have any intention of using them. Case decisions have also shown that it is enough if invoices or their supporting documents, sales reports (daily or otherwise prepared), weekly status reports or customer questionnaires are transmitted per distributor contract to a marketing firm retained by the manufacturer or importer.

Manufacturers and importers who wish to avoid the very negative consequences of the analogous application of Par. 89b HGB requiring a compensatory payment for the loss of customers must pay very strict attention to the drafting of the distributor contract. In particular, the contract must expressly state that the manufacturer (or importer) has no interest in the transmission of customers and the reasons why this is so.

If, however, the authorized distributor is contractually bound to transmit customers then, like the law pertaining to commercial agents, authorized-distributor law provides that the distributor's right to a compensatory payment cannot be contractually excluded. In order to preserve this claim, however, the authorized distributor must, like the commercial agent, raise it within one year following the termination of the distributor contract. Moreover, as with commercial agents, authorized distributors who terminate their contract due to age or sickness and for whom the continuation of their sales work would be unreasonable are entitled to compensatory payments for the loss of customers. If the manufacturer terminates the distributor contract, the compensatory payment is excluded only if the termination was based on serious cause.

The calculation of the amount of the compensatory payment for the loss of customers is made in essentially the same manner as described above in connection with commercial agents. In the case of authorized distributors, however, it is especially important to reduce the compensatory amount based on fairness reasons in order to account for that portion of the product's market appeal which is attributable to the manufacturer's (or importer's) advertising expenses. As a rule, this will result in the compensatory amount being reduced by 25%.

CHAPTER 8

COMPUTER LAW

Michael Karger

I. Protection of Computer Software

A. Applicable German laws

As in the United States, the question of how computer software rights can best be protected has long been the subject of debate in Germany. Instead of enacting a specific law designed for software, Germany has followed the lead of the U.S. to a large extent and determined that software rights are to be protected by copyright laws. Assuming certain requirements are met, software is also protected by patent and antitrust laws. Protection of the product name is provided by trademark law, which was most recently amended by the Trademark Act of 1996 ("Markengesetz").

Although the provisions of these individual areas of law work together to provide quite extensive protection for software, this protection is not without some gaps. The legal interplay of copyright, patent, antitrust and trademark law is complicated and not always easy to understand.

1. Copyright law

The most important protection for software is afforded by the German Copyright Act ("Urhebergesetz"). This law was amended in 1993 in order to conform to the European Council Directive of 1991 regarding the legal protection of computer programs. In its amended form, the law ensures that nearly all computer programs that demonstrate a minimum of intellectual creativity are protected. Prior to this amendment, the Federal Court ("Bundesgerichtshof") had required that software meet stringent criteria before it was entitled to protection. It ruled that only programs demonstrating an especially high degree of creativity were capable of being protected.

Similar to U.S. law, German copyright law protects only the "manifestations" (referred to in German as the "Ausdrucksformen") of a computer program. The ideas and principles upon which it is based are not protected.

A copyright originates with the creation of the software and expires seventy years after the death of its author. Registration of the copyright is neither necessary for its creation nor its enforcement.

Also, as under U.S. copyright law, owners of copyrights under German law are said to possess a "bundle of rights." They have the right to copy, revise and distribute the software. Nevertheless, it should be noted that by law there are certain uses that a copyright owner cannot prevent authorized users from making of the program. For example, the authorized user is entitled to make a back-up copy of the program, to test the functions of the program in order to understand the ideas and principles upon which it is based and to undertake measures to correct any mistakes in the program. If certain requirements are met, the user may also perform a decompilation of the program (separate it into its distinct parts). The rights granted by law to the authorized users of the program may not be altered by contract, and, thus, provisions in licensing contracts which attempt to strip users of their legal rights are void.

2. Patent law

The criteria which must be met in order for software to be protected under patent law are substantially more difficult to meet than under copyright law. Therefore, in practice, relatively few persons or companies apply for the issuance of a patent for their software-related inventions.

Under German law, programs for data-processing systems are clearly not viewed as patentable inventions. An invention, however, which otherwise meets the requirements of the patent law is not rendered unpatentable just because one of its parts is a computer program. In this case, the entire invention -- including the program -- is entitled to a patent. In order to receive a patent, the invention must involve a technology which meets the criterion of originality, be based on inventive activity and be commercially useful.

Patentable, for instance, are:

- inventions related to computer programs which change the composition or use of a data-processing system

  - or -

- inventions which relate to the data-processing system's ability to function and, in doing so, direct the way in which the technical elements of the data-processing program work together.

The types of computer program-related inventions capable of being patented therefore particularly include operation-system programs, programs which concern measuring and norm technology and programs for the processing of digital pictures or signals.

On the other hand, programs for such tasks as inventory administration, accounting, calculation or word processing are not patentable under German law because they do not demonstrate the requisite technical characteristics.

The right to the invention and the right to be granted a patent belong to the inventor. In order to be granted a patent, the inventor must register the invention with the Patent Office ("Patentamt"): The rights which derive from the patent end with the patent's expiration date which, as a rule, is twenty years from the date of it issuance. The owner of a patent has an exclusive right to it and can, for example, prohibit another from using the process or the results derived by using it.

3. Trade Secret Protection

Practice has shown that after copyright law, antitrust law is the next most important source of protection for computer software. According to the Unfair Competition Act ["Gesetz gegen den unlauteren Wettbewerb" (UWG)], it is illegal to expropriate the achievement of another

- when that achievement has significant impact on competition,
- when it involved considerable costs

  - and -
- when such expropriation or take-over amounts to depriving the owner (for example, a software writer) of the fruits of personal labor.

It is therefore illegal to make copies of computer programs and offer them on the market.

The Unfair Competition Act prohibits the unauthorized exploitation of business and trade secrets. Computer software can represent a protected business secret when the information in the program is not information which is otherwise readily available. This means that the secret contained in the software must be such that other persons do not have access to it or can achieve access to it only with considerable difficulty. Protected are, in particular, the "programming secrets." Antitrust law thus protects the entire spectrum of confidential technical know-how including the ideas that form the foundation of such know-how. To the extent and at the point where the secrets are publicly known, however, trade secret protection is lost.

4. Trademark Law

According to the new trademark law which was enacted in 1996, all marks which are designed to distinguish one product or service from another are capable of being protected. This includes but is not limited to words, pictures, word-and-picture combinations and sounds. In order to be protected the distinguishing mark must be registered in the trademark register and actually used in the marketplace. If the trademark is not used for a period of five years, it can be challenged. The owner of the trademark has the right to its exclusive use and can therefore prevent others from using it. The protection afforded by a trademark registered in Germany extends throughout the entire country and is valid for ten years from the date of the application filing. The term of protection can be extended for another ten years by paying an additional fee, and this process can be repeated as often as the owner wishes.

B. Applicable European Community laws

The European Community strives for standardization of the national laws of the Member States that provide protection for computer software rights. In the long run, this standardization will occur in all the areas of law discussed above. At the current time, however, more progress has been made in some areas than in others.

1. Copyright law

Although considerable differences exist between the general copyright laws of the Member States, much progress has been made in the specific area of computer software and data-bank protection. A 1991 European Council directive concerning the legal protection of computer programs requires all Member States to bring their laws into compliance with its provisions. Germany incorporated the directive's provisions into its national law in 1993. This directive requires that the Member States adopt certain minimum rules in order that a similar level of computer software protection be achieved throughout the Community. Such minimum rules ensure that the exclusive right of the copyright owner includes the right to prohibit others from copying or revising the software and distributing it to the public. On the other hand, the directive also requires that Member States adopt provisions which ensure that an authorized user has the right to make a back-up copy of the program. It is important to note that certain of the owner's rights arising from the copyright are exhausted upon the sale of the software program within the European Community.

In March of 1996, the European Parliament and Council passed Directive 96/9/EG, which concerns the protection of data banks. It requires Member States to incorporate its provisions into their national law by January 1, 1998.

Until recently, copyright protection for data banks was not available because they weren't generally seen as representing the requisite degree of intellectual creativity with respect to the range and arrangement of data. Now, however, because of Directive 96/9/EG, an independent protection system for data banks has been developed which requires only that a certain amount of originality in its compilation be present.

The person or company entitled to a specific data bank receives the exclusive rights to copy and revise it as well as the right to control its distribution. In addition, the owner can prohibit the "unfair" use of material contained in the data bank. The incorporation of Directive 96/9/EG into the Member States' national laws will be of significant importance to the multimedia industries.

At the current time, only a draft of a directive establishing a standard duration of a copyright exists. This proposed directive contains a provision that European copyrights are valid for seventy years following the death of the author.

2. Patent law

The European Patent Agreement of 1977 forms the authoritative basis for the European Community patent law. As a result of this agreement, the European Patent Office ("Europäisches Patentamt") was established in Munich. This office serves as the central administrative agency responsible for conducting the research and investigation necessary for the issuance of a European patent. The patents issued by the European Patent Office are valid throughout Europe from the date of their issuance but are simultaneously subject to the differing patent laws of the individual Member States. For this reason, one can say that no standard European Community patent currently exists.

The requirements for the granting of a patent according to the European Patent Agreement of 1977 are essentially the same as the requirements for the issuance of a patent under German law. It is expected that the European Patent Agreement will be replaced sometime in the future with an agreement that establishes unified protection throughout the entire Community, although no exact time has as yet been specified.

3. Trademark Law

In 1988, the European Council enacted a regulation pertaining to trademarks which resulted in an important change. It established uniform European-wide trademark protection which is effective in all the Member States. European Trademark Law is administered by the European Trademark Office in Alicante, Spain. One can apply for and receive a trademark only for the entire European Community. If issued, the trademark is effective throughout the Community; if declared invalid, it is likewise invalid throughout the Community. The regulations provide a protection time period of ten years and require that the trademark must be used to remain protected.

II. Procedures in the Event of an Infringement of Software Rights

The owners of computer software are entitled to seek judicial relief if their rights are violated. As in the U.S., it is possible for the owners of software rights in Germany to receive speedy interim relief in the form of a judicial order enjoining an infringement. The application for such a temporary injunction ("einstweilige Verfügung") does not require the payment of a bond. In the main action, the plaintiff may sue for a final order prohibiting the infringement as well as for damages and the surrender of any property of the defendant that constitutes the infringement.

In many respects, the infringement proceeding in Germany is subject to different civil rules of procedure than those applicable in U.S. legal proceedings. For example, under the German rules of civil procedure, no right to pretrial discovery (as that term is understood in U.S. jurisprudence) exists. The owners of software rights cannot compel defendants to give them evidence of the documents in their possession. As a result, proving an infringement is often difficult, especially in cases in which the plaintiff needs the source code of the other party in order to prove that the original program is identical with the program of the defendant.

Since, in contrast to the U.S. civil process, there is no trial by jury in Germany, all the evidence is reviewed and the legal issues decided by the judge. And, whereas the parties' experts play an important role in the U.S., they are of limited importance in determining the outcome of a German court case. If judges are unable to answer technical questions themselves, they call in an independent court expert ("Sachverständiger"), whose opinion, as a rule, is accepted by the Court. The testimony of the parties' own experts is usually given very little weight. Another important difference from the U.S. judicial system is the possibility of conducting two fact-finding procedures (trials) in Germany, which is to say that in an appeal evidence can once again be presented.

In summary, it can be said that the protection of software rights in Germany is essentially the same as the protection afforded under U.S. law. Nevertheless, many considerable differences exist concerning procedural details. Not all of the well-known principles of U.S. law will be automatically recognized in Germany.

III. Software and Computer Contracts

A. General principles

Under German law, the parties are free to determine the terms of their computer software or hardware contract as they see fit. If the contracting party located in Germany is a merchant ("Kaufmann") as that term is clearly defined by law, it is possible to agree that the contract will be governed by U.S. rather than German law. Nevertheless, German contracting parties often are not willing to accept the contracts drafted by U.S. firms.

If the contract is to be subject to German law, then, particularly in the case of standard contracts or standard-contract terms, care should be taken to ensure compliance with consumer-protection laws. If this is not done, it is possible that certain provisions of the contract could later be deemed invalid. For example, contract clauses which limit or exclude liability are often found to violate consumer-protection laws and are therefore declared unenforceable. In such a case, the party that attempted to avoid liability will be declared fully liable.

Software and hardware are subject to German product liability laws. According to these laws, the manufacturer (and under certain circumstances the importer and seller) are liable for defects in the product. This liability cannot be ruled out by contract.

Public contracting authorities (public agencies, hospitals and public utilities) are often willing to accept only certain standard contracts. Such contracts typically give them advantages over the contractor. One often finds these standard contracts or contract terms in contracts for the purchase, rent and servicing of hardware as well as for the development, licensing and maintenance of software.

To the extent that the parties do not expressly address an issue in their contract, then the terms of the German laws, in particular those of the Civil Code (BGB), the Commercial Code (HGB) and the Copyright Act (UrhG) apply. If the parties do not wish to deviate from the provisions of German law, the issue need not be addressed in the contract at all, which generally tends to keep German contracts shorter than their U.S. counterparts.

B. Licensing and distribution contracts

In drafting licensing or distribution contracts for software, the parties must observe the mandatory antitrust laws. A violation of such laws results in the invalidity of the contract. The Law Against Restraint on Competition (GWB) makes any terms in licensing contracts problematical when they attempt to restrain the use and application of software, prohibit sublicensing and assignment or require the coupling of the software to certain other software programs.

German law does not permit distribution contracts to require independent distributors to enter sublicensing contracts with the end users at specific prices or according to certain conditions. All contracts which contain limiting provisions relating to antitrust law must be in writing. If not reduced to writing, then the contract is unenforceable.

The European antitrust law is in many respects stricter than the German antitrust law (see Chapter 10). The most important European antitrust provisions are Art. 85 and 86 of the Treaty Establishing the European Economic Community (EEC Treaty). Article 85 prohibits agreements between enterprises which prohibit, limitate or distort competition within the European Community. Such agreements are unenforceable. A violation of Article 85 can subject the enterprises to heavy fines. According to Article 85 (3), an enterprise whose contract contains a limitation on competition can apply to the European Commission for an exemption. Although the Commission is empowered to provide exemptions if certain conditions are met, the process is not always practical and often quite drawn out. For that reason the Commission has passed several regulations which exempt certain categories of contracts ("block exemptions").

With respect to software and hardware, the European Commission regulation regarding contracts for the transfer of technology, which came into effect on April 4, 1996, should be mentioned. This regulation removes computer software and hardware contracts from the coverage of block exemptions No. 2349/84 regarding patent licensing agreements and No. 556/89 regarding know-how agreements. This transfer of technology regulation applies to pure patent licenses; that means, it covers licenses to national patents issued by the Member States as well as licenses to Community and European patents. In addition, the regulation applies to pure know-how agreements. Such agreements are license agreements to technical knowledge which are not protected by a patent as well as mixed patent and know-how license agreements. Finally, the regulation is applicable to pure or mixed agreements that grant a license to patents or know-how and also contain a license for other intellectual property rights (in particular trademarks, registered designs and copyrights) if such an additional license contributes to the realization of the purpose of the transferred technology and contains collateral clauses.

Article 86 also contains significant European antitrust law. It prohibits the abuse of a market-controlling position in the Community to the extent this abuse could have a negative effect on trade between the Member States.

The European Court of Justice issued a decision on April 6, 1995 which could prove to have considerable impact on contracts pertaining to protected software (Magill, RTE and ITP versus Commission). In this decision, the Court held that the owner's use of an exclusive right could, under exceptional conditions, amount to an abuse of a controlling marketing position. This is the case if the owner has, in fact, a monopoly on certain information. This opinion could possibly lead to a situation in which owners with a monopoly on important technology must make their know-how available to the market. This could apply particularly to certain firms which place standard-setting products on the market. One must wait and see how the European Court of Justice case law continues to develop in this area.

CHAPTER 9

ENFORCEMENT OF RIGHTS AND CLAIMS THROUGH THE COURTS AND ARBITRATION TRIBUNALS / THE GERMAN NOTARY AND ATTORNEY FEES

Reinhard Nacke

I. Judicial Resolution of Disputes

A. Overview of Germany's system of courts

In comparison to many other countries, the judicial system in Germany is characterized by a relatively large number and variety of courts. The reasons for this are the existence of several appeal levels for nearly every dispute, and the fact that specialized courts have been created to handle certain legal categories of disputes. Generally, plaintiffs may file a lawsuit in one of two courts. For civil actions, in which the matter in dispute is DM 10,000.-- or less, the Local Court ("Amtsgericht") has jurisdiction in the first instance and all appeals must be filed in the Regional Court ("Landgericht"). In civil actions in which the matter in dispute exceeds DM 10,000.--, original jurisdiction lies with the Regional Court and appellate jurisdiction with the Regional Court of Appeals ("Oberlandesgericht") and possibly (particularly in cases involving large monetary disputes) in the Federal Supreme Court ("Bundesgerichtshof").

For certain legal actions, however, original jurisdiction lies with specialized courts; appeals from such courts' decisions must then be filed in specialized appellate courts.

Cases brought before the Commercial Division of the Regional Court and the Labor Courts are decided by a panel made up of professional judges and citizens known as "lay judges" ("Laienrichter"). In Labor Court proceedings, these judges are recommended by employer and employee organizations. In matters before the Commercial Division of the Regional Court, the lay judges are citizens who have been recommended by the Chamber of Industry and Commerce ["Industrie- und Handelskammer" (IHK)]. The input of these lay judges often helps to ensure that the economic background of a case is considered in the decision-making process. A preference for arbitration over judicial resolution of a dispute on the basis that the courts lack economic or commercial expertise is, therefore, unjustified (see II. below regarding arbitration tribunals).

The highest appellate court in Germany's judicial system is the Federal Constitutional Court ("Bundesverfassungsgericht"). This court is not only empowered to resolve issues submitted to it by one of Germany's states or by the Parliament ("Bundestag"), but also hears appeals from citizens who

- claim that their constitutional rights have been violated

  - and -

- can show that no other means of protecting those constitutional rights exist.

B. Length of time from filing of complaint to judgment

The time between the filing of a complaint and final judgment can vary greatly from case to case. Often, in those lawsuits where one might even prefer a longer process, a final judgment is pronounced in two or three months, while in other cases in which the client strongly desires a speedy decision, the process can take years and involve at least two appellate levels.

Nevertheless, it can be generally said that if a lawsuit involves relatively clear facts, a final judgment can usually be obtained in less than six months. On the other hand, in legal disputes which are highly contested, complicated and involve large amounts of money, one cannot usually expect a trial court judgment until after more than one year. Experience has proven, however, that the time from initiation until conclusion of the judicial process is shorter in Germany than in other countries.

One reason for this could be the fact that the oral and documentary evidence submitted to the court is limited. While in many countries the parties must present the court with all documents and facts which have a relationship to their case, in Germany, each party determines which facts to provide the court and its opposing party. This means, as well, that there is no "pre-trial discovery" as that term is understood in the USA.

Moreover, in making its decision, the court must disregard facts which the parties themselves have agreed shall not be considered in resolving their dispute. The court must also accept the truth of any facts presented by one party which the other party has failed to challenge- even if the court has doubts about the correctness of such facts.

This limitation on the amount of oral and documentary information used during litigation leads to a simplification and reduction in time of the judicial process. In addition, it often results in the attorney's litigation strategy being a deciding factor in how the court resolves a dispute. On the other hand, however, if the attorney conducts the litigation in a careless or negligent manner, the court, being restricted in the information it may consider, often has no choice but to rule against the party represented by such attorney. The attorney, therefore, shoulders a large responsibility for ensuring that the litigation is properly conducted.

C. Accelerated relief

Accelerated relief is possible, for example:

- in actions filed with the above mentioned Commercial Division of the Regional Court
- to enforce certain specified types of legal instruments (for example, checks and promissory notes)

  - or -

- to initiate a special, largely automatic summary proceeding for debt recovery known as a "Mahnverfahren."

This last referenced summary proceeding is conducted primarily through the filing of forms and enables a plaintiff with a monetary claim which is uncontested to quickly and relatively inexpensively obtain a final judgment. The Local Court for Berline-Schöneberg generally handles the "Mahnverfahren" brought by foreign claimants; for non-foreign claimants, the residence or domicile of the claimant determines which Local Court has jurisdiction.

In addition, when a plaintiff can show that without such relief a danger of irreparable damage exists, accelerated relief is also possible to achieve either through the use of what is known as a "freeze order" ("Arrest") or through an application for a preliminary injunction. Through such proceedings, the plaintiff can- within days or even hours- obtain accelerated relief in the form, for example, of a judicial order prohibiting the defendant from disposing of property or from engaging in certain conduct.

It is important to note, however, that accelerated relief through a freeze order or an application for a preliminary injunction will not be granted merely upon a showing that without such relief a defendant/debtor would be unable to pay a future judgment; rather, it must be shown that the debtor is attempting or has attempted to conceal property, or that as a result of a criminal offense, there is a suspicion that this could be the case. Finally, these procedures are not designed to conclusively determine the respective rights of the parties to a dispute. Only relief of a temporary nature- which can, if necessary, be later rescinded- is available. Any seized money or property will not be turned over immediately to the creditor; rather, it will be held in safe-keeping until the conclusion of the litigation.

Generally, it can be said, that the initiation of such an "Arrest" proceeding or the application for a preliminary injunction raises the legal costs considerably due to the possibility that the same dispute must be concurrently litigated in two proceedings- with each proceeding affording several levels of appellate review.

An additional way in which accelerated relief may be obtained is through a settlement arranged by the parties' attorneys in accordance with § 1044 b of the "Zivilprozeßordnung" (Rules of Civil Procedure). When certain requirements are met, such a settlement is enforceable just like a judgment of a court. If the debtor fails to pay the amount agreed to in the settlement, then said settlement can be enforced in the way described below.

In addition, it is possible for a debtor to declare in a document which has been approved by a German notary that said document is acknowledged as executory title (§ 794 par. 1 No. 5 of the “Zivilprozeßordnung”). This means that the debtor acknowledges that the document is one which justifies execution.

Naturally, these last two possibilities can only be used with the debtor’s agreement. For this reason, their use is limited to situations where the parties’ respective legal rights are very clear or where one party makes his entering into of a contract dependent on the providing of such a declaration by the other party. Particularly in transactions involving the sale of real property or ownership interests in a business, it is not unusual for the buyer to declare in a notarized sales contract that he acknowledges the document to be subject to enforcement proceedings.

D. Enforcement of judgments

The enforcement of monetary judgments is undertaken by a sheriff’s officer (“Gerichtsvollzieher”) when such enforcement involves the seizure of personal property. When, however, the seizure of receivables or real property is involved, the enforcement proceeding must be handled by the court.

Usually, the enforcement procedure can be initiated immediately after the rendering of a judgment, and this is true even if the opposing party has the possibility to appeal the judgment. Often, however, before or immediately following the enforcement, the creditor must deposit a security to cover the time period in which avenues of appeal remain available to the debtor. Usually, the security is in the form of a bank guarantee.

A creditor who is enforcing a claim for money most often attempt to have the debtor's bank accounts or regular income seized. Another possibility is the attachment of the debtor's personal or real property. One disadvantage of the enforcement procedure is that the creditor must decide which of these types of assets he wishes to first pursue; pursuing several enforcement measures at the same time is not possible for practical reasons (the original judgment must be presented each time).

If the enforcement procedure is unsuccessful, the creditor can make a motion that the debtor provide a so-called "Offenbarungsversicherung" (§§ 807, 899 et. seq. "Zivilprozeßordnung"). In such a document, the debtor must verify under oarth whether and if so what property he or she possesses. The fact that the debtor has provided an "Offenbarungsversicherung" is noted in a register maintained by the Local Court which has jurisdiction in the geographical area containing the debtor's residence or domicile (§ 915 "Zivilprozeßordnung").

This register is open to the public; therefore, its entries typically find their way into the information pages of, for example, credit reporting businesses or the Chamber of Industry and Commerce. The entry thus results in the debtor having difficulty in continuing his self-employment or employment activity. In this way, the "Offenbarungsversicherung" places a pressure on those debtors, for whom the possibility of raising the funds exists, to satisfy their debts.

On the other hand, it can also occur that the debtor uses his "Offenbarungsversicherung" to fend off his creditors; then, he obtains employment, for example, in his wife's business and receives an income which is not subject to attachment. This is possible because whereas all monthly income of a single person over 1,209.00 DM is subject to attachment (assuming he has no support obligations), the amount of income which is not subject to seizure increases depending on the number of persons which the debtor must support. In this way, therefore, sometimes a person, despite his large amount of debt, can enjoy a relatively comfortable standard of living.

Due to multilateral and bilateral international agreements, judgments of foreign courts and arbitration tribunals are, in theory, just as enforceable in Germany as are the judgments of German courts and arbitration tribunals. Nevertheless, holders of foreign judgments are first required to obtain an order from a German court confirming the enforceability of the particular foreign judgment (§§ 722 et. seq. "Zivilprozeßordnung").

Although the judge does not review the underlying factual or legal correctness of the foreign judgment during this German enforcement proceeding, such proceeding usually lasts quite a long time and results in additional costs. Moreover, there is always the risk that the foreign judgment will fail to meet German legal requirements and therefore be declared "unenforceable". For these reasons, in many cases it is advisable (assuming such court is, according to German law, competent to hear the matter) to file the original complaint in the German court.

E. Court costs and attorney fees

In principle, for lawsuits in which the monetary value of the matters in dispute is the same and which are pursued to the same stage of judicial proceeding, the costs are the same throughout Germany. This is due to the existence of statutes which regulate both attorney fees ["Bundesrechtsanwaltsgebühren-ordnung" (BRAGO)] and court costs ["Gerichtskostengesetz" (GKG)]. These laws provide, in part, that regardless of the <u>actual</u> court and attorney time or difficulty of a case, attorney fees and court costs increase depending on

- the monetary value of the matter in dispute

  - and -

- the stage of the judicial process the lawsuit reaches (for example: filing of complaint, filing of motion(s), hearing of evidence, settlement, judgment, appeal).

Below are three examples in which these primary cost-determining factors are illustrated. The cost figures include court costs, the costs of the client's own attorney(s), the costs of the opponent's attorney(s) and value-added tax. Although an expert witness ("Sachverständiger") is often deemed necessary and, therefore, appointed by the court, this cost is not included in the figures below; it should be kept in mind however, that such additional cost may also arise. Finally, it should be noted that the inclusion of value-added tax can result in a slight overstatement of the costs for many clients because it is not always necessary to include it in an invoice; moreover, even when it is included, it does not represent a real cost for those business clients who are entitled to deduct the VAT they have paid to their attorney from the amount they have collected from their customers and would otherwise be required to transmit to the tax department.

	Amount in Dispute: DM 20,000.	Amount in Dispute: DM 200,000.
1. one court involved; no hearing of evidence (i.e., no examination of witnesses; no expert witness); no settlement	DM 5,600.--	DM 18,080.--
2. one court involved; hearing of evidence; settlement	DM 9,180.--	DM 27,290.--
3. two courts involved (appeal); no hearing of evidence; no settlement	DM 13,080.--	DM 42,610.--

These examples indicate that, in relation to the amount in dispute, the costs increase digressively rather than progressively. In other words, smaller amounts in dispute lead to proportionately higher costs whereas higher amounts in dispute carry with them proportionately lower costs. If, for example, the amount in dispute in example number three above was raised to DM 2 million, then the costs would only be DM 164,580.--.

The reason that the costs include the fee for the client's own attorney as well as the attorney of the opponent is because, as a rule, such costs are divided between the plaintiff and the defendant depending on the extent one or the other has prevailed in the lawsuit. For example, if a party loses on all issues, then that party must pay all costs and the prevailing party is in turn relieved of the cost burden. [Note: in Labor Court proceedings in the first instance (not on appeal), each party bears their own costs regardless of the outcome].

This rule that the prevailing party is fully reimbursed for costs is only applicable when the party's attorneys have calculated their fees in accordance with the "Attorney Fees Ordinance" (BRAGO), which, with respect to business clients, tends often not to be the case. Since many commercial legal matters involve international facts and issues or an unusually long judicial process, it is not unusual for the attorneys and clients involved in such matters to enter into fee agreements which deviate from the fees fixed by law. Often an hourly fee arrangement is agreed to. The amount of this hourly fee varies depending on the region, the law firm, the importance of the case, etc. Roughly speaking, however, fees agreed to by special contract usually currently range from between DM 350.-- and DM 700.-- per hour. If the attorney costs of prevailing parties have been agreed to by private contract and exceed the fees fixed by law, then such parties are only entitled to be reimbursed for the costs in the amount allowed by statute. They must pay anything in excess of that amount themselves.

Of course, it can also occur that the attorney costs calculated on an hourly basis are actually less than the statutory fee. This could be the case, for instance, if the lawsuit is resolved very early on in the process. If this happens, however, the attorney must bill the client at the higher statutory rate because he is ethically and legally obliged not to undercut the attorneys' fees set by statute.

Any type of contingent fee arrangement is strictly prohibited in Germany.

It is important to note that the plaintiff must pay court costs in advance and that this advance payment must include payment for all stages of the judicial proceeding which the lawsuit could theoretically reach. If the lawsuit is resolved at an earlier stage, a refund is provided. In the above three examples, court costs for the lawsuits with a monetary value of DM 20,000.-- would be DM 1,150.--; and for the lawsuits worth DM 200,000.--, the court costs would be DM 5,265.--.

In addition, it is customary for the attorney to require a reasonable retainer ("Vorschuß"). This is an advance payment of fees and is allowed under the "Attorney Fees Ordinance" (§17). Plaintiffs from foreign countries can also be required to provide a security deposit to cover the possibility of losing the law suit, in which case they would be obliged to pay the defendant's costs (§ 110 "Zivilprozeßordnung").

Many persons, and as a matter of fact, particularly private persons, are not affected by court costs and attorney fees. Such persons are insured against the costs of legal disputes. This legal costs insurance covers the costs of the insured party's own attorney, court costs as well as the costs of the opposing party.

II. Use of Arbitration Tribunals to Resolve Disputes

It is becoming more and more common in commercial disputes to turn to arbitration tribunals rather than to the courts. Parties sometimes use the arbitration services of the Arbitration Tribunal of the International Chamber of Commerce in Paris. Usually, however, they submit their disputes to arbitrators who have been appointed by one of the following:

- the Chamber of Industry and Commerce,
- appellate judges (for example, the Chief of the Regional Court of Appeals for a particular city)

  - or -
- organizations such as the "German Arbitration Institute" in Cologne or the "German Arbitration Committee" in Bonn.

The reasons that parties often agree to arbitration of potential future disputes include cost and time savings as well as the greater confidentiality which an arbitration process affords (unlike a court hearing, an arbitration hearing can be closed). The fact of the matter is, however, that the first objective is often not realized. Once an actual dispute arises, parties frequently spend much time debating whether the dispute is of the type they initially agreed to submit to arbitration and/or arguing over the choice of an arbitrator.

The parties can also find themselves disappointed by the costs of the arbitration process. Because many arbitration agreements specify the appointment of a decision-making panel comprised of three arbitrators, the costs of the arbitration process (particularly in the case of disputes involving relatively low monetary values) can be higher than court costs.

The point here, however, is not to dissuade parties from entering into arbitration agreements but rather to emphasize the importance of exercising great care in the drafting of such agreements. If this is done, arbitration often remains a more efficient and satisfactory dispute-resolution method than the courts.

III. Notary Fees

The notary's position often varies from state to state. In the states of Bavaria, Saxony and parts of Rhineland-Westphalia, for example, there is what is called a "pure notary," or a person who functions only as a notary. In Hessen, Schleswig-Holstein, Lower Saxony and parts of Rhineland-Westphalia, on the other hand, the person who functions as a notary may also work as an attorney. In Baden-Württemberg, the notary public is a civil servant.

One thing that these various forms of notaries have in common, however, is that all are subject to the laws which regulate their legal activities and their fees.

The functions of the notary are regulated in a multitude of statutory provisions. Generally, it can be said that the notary is responsible for authenticating signatures and certifying that legal transactions- in particular contracts- meet the requirements imposed by law in order for them to be effective.

With an authentication, the notary is only attesting that a signature was made in his presence by a person who has provided the notary with proof that he bears the same name and identity as that reflected in the signature.

With the certification that a transaction is in the form and otherwise meets the requirements imposed by law, the notary is himself responsible for the preparation of the entire document. This does not necessarily mean that he has drafted the contract or other document. He must, however, sign the document just like the other parties. In addition, he must read the entire contract aloud to the parties, even if it is very long (§ 13 "Beurkundungsgesetz"). The notary is also obliged to inform the parties about the meaning of the contract and its associated risks (§ 17

"Beurkundungsgesetz"). In so doing, the notary is naturally prohibited from favoring one party or the other. Persons who wish to ensure that their interests- for example, their interests in a contract- are protected usually commission their own attorney either to draft the contract or to review the contract drafted by the opposing side or the notary. If the notary has no concerns regarding the contract presented by the parties, he will, as a rule certify the contract. As a precaution, however, the notary should be informed in advance if an attorney has been commissioned to prepare the draft (in the event the notary is already involved at this stage of the negotiations).

As noted above, requirements that transactions be approved by a notary can be found in many laws. The most important transactions requiring notarization include contracts for the sale of real property [§ 313 "Bürgerliches Gesetzbuch" or BGB (Civil Code)] and contracts for the sale of ownership interests in a GmbH (§ 15 "GmbH Gesetz"). Also requiring notarization, however, are gifts (§ 518 BGB), marriage contracts (§ 1410 BGB), articles of incorporation of a stock corporation [§ 23 "Aktiengesetz" (Stock Law)] or of a limited liability company (§ 2 "GmbH Gesetz").

In order to perform the above described functions in a competent manner, it is important that notaries have a solid legal background. In fact, notaries in Germany first receive the same education as judges and attorneys before going on to complete a special educational program designed for notaries.

The fees of notaries are regulated by the "Kostenordnung" (KostO). Similar to the Attorneys' Fees Ordinance (BRAGO), this statute provides that the fees of notaries are determined by the type of work performed and the value of the underlying transaction, whose legality they are requested to certify. For example, the charge for the certification of a contract which establishes a GmbH with original capital of DM 50,000.-- or for the certification of a contract for the sale of equity holdings in a GmbH for DM 50,000.-- is the same: DM 320.--. If, however, the very same contracts are involved, with the sole difference that the value of the underlying transaction is one million German marks instead of DM 50,000.--, the charge is DM 3220.--. Not included in this fee are postal charges as well as the costs of any extra document preparation not covered by the statutory fee. Finally, the types of notary contracts in the above examples often entail separate costs for an attorney and/or tax adviser who prepares the underlying documents or submits them to the notary.

Notaries are subject to stricter regulation with regards to their fees than either attorneys, certified accountants or tax advisers. For example, notaries are not allowed to enter into a fee agreement which provides for a different fee than that fixed by law. For this reason, when the value of the underlying transaction is very high, parties often look for a foreign notary whose fees are lower.

Chapter 10

INSTITUTIONS OF THE EUROPEAN COMMUNITY

Bernd Tremml

I. Overview

The tasks entrusted to the European Community are carried out by five institutions: the Council of Ministers, the Commission, the European Parliament, the Court of Justice and the Court of Auditors. The most important of these is the Council, in which the most significant governmental functions have been combined. The Council is primarily responsible for passing laws and making the decisions necessary to realize the goals of the Treaty Establishing the European Community as amended (EC Treaty), as well as other treaties. The Council consists of representatives of the governments from each Member State. Because all of the Council Ministers have a duty to follow the instructions of their government, the Council's decisions have the effect of reconciling the differing national interests.

The Council of Ministers is designed as a body whose function is to represent the interests of the individual Member States. The Commission consists of twenty citizens of the Member States who are first nominated by the States and then, following a vote of approval by the European Parliament as a whole, appointed by common accord of the Member States. The Commission must include at least one citizen from each Member State but may not include more than two members from the same State.

In contrast to the Council, the functions of the Commission are primarily executive rather than legislative, although it does play an authoritative role in shaping Community policy and in the legislative process in general. For example, only the Commission, is empowered to submit proposed legislation to the Council. The Commission is also in charge of the Community's extensive administrative apparatus. If a Member State fails to comply with Community law, the Commission can institute enforcement proceedings and, as a last resort, file a complaint with the European Court of Justice.

Another important institution of the European Community is the European Parliament. The Parliament consists of representatives of the Member States who are elected by direct universal suffrage. Depending on the type of legislative proposal being considered by the Council, the Parliament is empowered to participate in the legislative process in one of two ways: either by giving its assent (without which such assent a proposal cannot become law), or by giving an advisory opinion, which is not binding on the Council.

The European Court of Justice, which is discussed in greater detail in III. below, consists of fifteen judges who possess the qualifications required for appointment to the highest judicial office in their respective countries. The Court is charged with the role of safeguarding and maintaining the rights and duties of the individual citizens and organizations as well as ruling on questions involving the legality, application and/or interpretation of Community law.

The Court of Auditors consists of fifteen members with proven auditing experience who are chosen from the population of the Member States. This institution is charged with the duty, among others, of examining the accounts of all revenues and expenditures of the Community.

II. Laws Enacted by the Council or Jointly by the Council and European Parliament

The treaties entered into by the Member States constitute the primary law of the Community. These treaties often empower the Community institutions to enact laws in order to further the treaties' goals. The law enacted by the Community institutions themselves is known as "secondary Community law" and usually takes the form of either a regulation or directive. A typical regulation or directive will be enacted by the Council upon the suggestion of the Commission and after either

- the Council has obtained the opinion of the Parliament, which they are not bound to follow,

  \- or -

- the Council has obtained the approval of the Parliament, without which approval enactment is impossible.

A. European Community regulations

According to Art. 189 paragraph 2 of the EC treaty, the regulations of the Community are binding in their entirety and directly applicable in all Member States. Direct applicability means that the regulation takes effect automatically upon being published in the Official Journal of the European Community. No further legislative action on the part of Member States is required. The only situation in which a delay in the effective date is allowed is, if the regulation necessitates the establishment by the States of their own administrative apparatus.

Community regulations have the effect of granting rights as well as imposing responsibilities on the governmental agencies, courts and natural or legal persons of the Member States. Any national law which conflicts with a Community regulation is rendered invalid and inapplicable.

B. European Community directives

As a general rule, directives are not directly applicable (see Art. 189 paragraphs 2 and 3 of the EC Treaty). Unlike regulations, they must be incorporated into the law of the Member States before they take effect. A Community directive gives the Member States the legislative goal to be achieved; the States then have a duty under Article 189 paragraph 3 to incorporate the directive's provisions into their national law. In so doing, the Member States cannot change the content of the directive. They are, however, given the discretion to determine the form and method of incorporation. Directives serve to harmonize the laws of the Member States. Regulations, on the other hand, lead to uniformity and standardization of the laws throughout the Community.

The general principle that a directive cannot be directly applied until acted on by the Member State has been considerably modified by the European Court of Justice. In line with its decisions regarding the direct applicability of primary law, the Court has held that under certain specific circumstances a directive is applicable without Member State action. According to the Court of Justice, the individual can seek direct application of a directive by the national courts, even if it is not yet a part of national law, if the requirements set forth in the Court's "Kolpinghuis" decision are met (Court of Justice, Rs. 80/86, Slg. 1987, 3969). The Court of Justice held in "Kolpinghuis" that the provisions of a directive can be directly applied if the Member State has not in a timely or sufficient manner incorporated the directive into its national law, <u>and</u> if the particular regulation in the directive in question is itself sufficiently exact and its content is unconditional.

Whether or not a directive has been incorporated into the Member State's national law in a timely fashion is usually easy to determine because most directives contain a provision stating when this must be accomplished. It is more difficult to prove that this same incorporation has not been performed sufficiently. This requires detailed arguments which show exactly how the national government fails to comply with the standards set by the directive.

A regulation in a directive is considered sufficiently clear or certain if it contains a clear and precise legal proposition. In other words, the regulation must contain a precise requirement that can stand alone without further action on the part of the Member State.

Finally, the content of a directive is unconditional if it can be applied and made effective without the necessity of the Member State passing additional rules or taking any additional action. A determination whether a directive is directly applicable must be made on a case by case basis. The rationale given by the Court of Justice for allowing the direct application of directives under the above outlined circumstances is that a Member State should not be allowed to circumvent its duties with regard to directives by an untimely and/or improper incorporation of the directive into its national law. If the people of a Member State could be derived of their individual rights granted by the Community's directives just because of the Member State's dereliction of duty, the practical effectiveness of directives would be limited or even completely frustrated. Moreover, direct applicability of directives helps to safeguard the effectiveness of the Community. The effect of the Court of Justice's decision has been to carve out another way, in addition to the Breach of Treaty Proceeding of Article 169 of the EC Treaty (discussed below), to sanction Member States who fail to timely and sufficiently incorporate directives into their own law.

The highest court of the Federal Republic of Germany (the Federal Constitutional Court [„Bundesverfassungsgericht"]) has upheld the Court of Justice's decision allowing for the direct applicability of directives. The Federal Constitutional Court has found the Court of Justice's decision to be a legitimate, constitutionally acceptable development of the law of the European Community.

III. Proceedings Conducted by the European Court of Justice

The European Court of Justice is located in Luxembourg. As mentioned above, the Court of Justice is charged with ensuring that the law is observed in the interpretation and application of the amended EC treaty as well as other primary and secondary legislation. The decision-making tribunal consisting of fifteen judges is served and supported by eight Advocates General. These Individuals neither represent a party to the proceeding nor are they members of the bench; rather, they serve as legal consultants to the

Court. Their position is similar in certain respects to that of a judge. The Advocates General are independent reporters of fact and law and are responsible solely for the upholding of Community law. The arguments they present to the Court of Justice must be predicated on the Advocates General's impartial and independent reasoning. As a result, their input in the cases pending before the Court of Justice helps to preserve the integrity of the basic principles of Community law and in particular, the consistent application of its case law.

The Court of Justice exercises its judicial function in various types of proceedings. In 1988, in order to ease the burdened Court of Justice, a Court of First Instance was created and given jurisdiction to hear and make decisions at the trial level, subject to a right of appeal to the Court of Justice on points of law. The Court of First Instance is not a new European Community institution; rather, it is a part of the Court of Justice. Both its administrative and budgetary structure is attached to that of the Court of Justice. Both courts are located in Luxembourg. One important difference between the courts, however, is that the Court of First Instance is not served by the Advocates General.

The method for establishing the Court of First Instance's specific jurisdiction is set forth in Article 168a of the EC Treaty which provides that the Council, upon request of the Court of Justice and following consultation with the European Parliament and the Commission, shall determine the classes of actions and proceedings the new Court will handle.

Initially, the Court of First Instance was given jurisdiction primarily over complaints of government employees, antitrust proceedings and actions to recover damages, but subsequently and due in part to the Maastricht Treaty, its jurisdiction has been considerably expanded to cover other types of matters as well. As the division of power between the two courts further develops, the Court of Justice will most likely continue to be responsible for Community matters involving the necessity of a uniform interpretation of Community law or decisions regarding the division of power between the Community and the Member States or between the Community organizations themselves. Cases bearing an administrative nature will increasingly tend to be the province of the Court of First Instance.

The sole type of proceeding which with certainty will not be assigned in the future to the Court of First Instance is the Preliminary Ruling Procedure under Article 177. An explanation of this proceeding as well as the equally important proceeding known as the Treaty Violation Proceeding follows. Both of these proceedings are provided in detail in the EC Treaty.

A. The Treaty Violation Proceeding

The Treaty Violation Proceeding of Article 169 of the EC Treaty can be used to punish a Member State for its violation of Community law. A violation of Community law is present when a Member State fails to fulfill an obligation under the various treaties, regulations, directives, etc. adopted pursuant to Community law. Either the Commission or another Member State (even when the Member State is not directly affected by the violation) may initiate a Treaty Violation Proceeding.

In its eleventh annual report regarding the enforcement of Community law, the Commission advised the European Parliament that 1340 alleged treaty violations were processed in 1993. Three hundred and eighty-three, or nearly 30%, of these violations fell under the jurisdiction of the Community Administrative Department in charge of environmental, nuclear safety and catastrophic event issues. The alleged violations involved either the insufficient incorporation of directives into national law or breaches of Community law.

Individual citizens or organizations are not entitled to file a Treaty Violation Proceeding with the Court of Justice. Citizens and groups do, however, have the right to provide the Commission with information alleging a treaty violation. The Commission in turn has a duty to follow up on all proper complaints.

A citizen complaint meets the Commission requirements if it is in writing and sufficiently concrete. The information that the citizen provides the Commission must point to a treaty violation with sufficient clarity. It is not necessary that the citizen show that he or she is personally damaged by the violation (i.e. that he is a neighbor, for example, who would directly benefit from the cessation of the violation). In order to make it easier for Community citizens to exercise their complaint rights, the Commission has published a complaint formula and has granted individuals specific procedural guarantees. Upon receipt of a proper complaint by a citizen or group, the Commission is then required to request the concerned country to respond to the complaint. If the Member State's response is insufficient, the Commission has the power to initiate a Treaty Violation Proceeding.

If a complaint alleging a treaty violation is proven, the Court of Justice merely declares that a violation has occurred. Acts which violate the Treaty will neither be set aside nor held to be illegal; nor will the Court specify what actions must be taken in order for the Member State in violation to come into compliance. Rather, the Member

State itself is required to determine the necessary compliance measures and to implent those measures. If subsequently, the Commission determines that the Member State has not done this, it may, after giving the State an opportunity to respond, issue an opinion which specifies how the Member State has failed to comply with the judgment of the Court of Justice. If the Member State still fails to come into compliance within the time specified in the Commission's opinion, the Commission may once again bring the matter before the Court of Justice and seek an order imposing a lump-sum penalty on the Member State. In order to prevail in a Treaty Violation Proceeding, it must be proven that the underlying act which constitutes a violation of Community law can be ascribed or imputed to the Member State (the Court looks at the legal situation at the point in time when the specified time period given the Member State to respond to the complaint expires).

1. Violations of law attributable to a Member State

From the perspective of Community law, a Member State is perceived as one uniform actor, which means that it is held responsible for all violations of Community law which are committed by subordinate institutions, agencies or bodies of the State which includes the national Parliament and members of the executive branch or its administrative offices. In countries with a federal system such as Germany, the Member State can also be held responsible when one of the legislative bodies of the states refuses to incorporate in a timely manner a Community directive into its own state-wide law. Actions (or failure to act) of private persons which constitute a violation of Community law, however, cannot be ascribed to the Member States unless the government bears some responsibility for the breach.

Recently a particular problem has developed with respect to national court decisions which either do not respect the priority of the Community law or fail to apply it even when it is directly relevant to the case. Because national courts derive their power from the Constitutions of the Member States, their actions can also be the basis of a violation on the part of a Member State.

Many persons, however, seriously question whether the initiation of a Treaty Violation Proceeding against a Member State based on the action of its court is a reasonable option. National courts are independent institutions. Even if the Court of Justice declares that a treaty violation has occurred, neither the national court nor any other branch of the Member State's government has the authority to set aside the national court's decision. The Court of Justice's decision in a Treaty Violation Proceeding can therefore at best have only a future influence on the national courts. In addition, the initiation of Treaty Violation Proceedings against Member States based on the decisions of their national courts would lead to considerable political difficulties between Member States and the European Community.

It should not be overlooked that, in addition to the Treaty Violation Proceeding, other options exist that can bring the national courts into compliance with Community law. For example, if a lower national court wishes to deviate from a higher court's opinion which it suspects violates Community law, Article 177 of the EC Treaty empowers the lower court to seek a preliminary ruling by the Court of Justice [see (2) below]. In this way, the lower court can ensure that a correct interpretation of Community law is applied to its case and at the same time can avoid being bound by higher national court determinations pertaining to the issue. The case pending before the lower court as well as all future cases are then bound by the Court of Justice's preliminary ruling.

In addition, a party adversely affected by a lower national court's failure to uphold Community law can make use of methods under German law to challenge the decision. According to German Federal Constitutional Court decisions, a court which violates its duty under Article 177 paragraph 3 of the EC Treaty (which requires national courts whose decision cannot be appealed to seek a preliminary ruling from the Court of Justice in certain specified matters involving interpretation of Community law), has simultaneously violated Art. 101 paragraph 1, sentence 2 of the German Constitution. On the basis of this violation of German Constitutional law, an aggrieved party is entitled to file a constitutional appeal of the national court's decision.

This check within German law for ensuring that Community law is followed has its limits. First, it requires that the party is harmed rather than advantaged by the national court's decision which violates Community law, and secondly, it is not an available option when it is Germany's highest court, the Federal Constitutional Court, whose decision violates Community law.

2. Breach of Treaty

In a Treaty Violation Proceeding, it must be proven that the Member State has "failed to fulfill an obligation under the Treaty." Despite the seemingly unequivocal wording of this EC Treaty provision, "an obligation under the Treaty" has been interpreted to refer not only to primary legislation such as treaties but also to secondary legislation such as regulations and directives, and to agreements of the

Community with third party States as well as to the general legal principles of the Community as interpreted by the Court of Justice.

A Member State has "failed to fulfill" its treaty obligations when it has either not applied Community law at all, incorrectly applied it, or has committed an act which constitutes an affirmative violation of a specific provision of Community law. The party who lodged the complaint (normally the Commission) has the burden of proof.

B. The Preliminary Ruling Proceeding

The Preliminary Ruling Proceeding under Art. 177 of the EC Treaty also plays an important role in Community affairs. To date, approximately one-half of all Court of Justice proceedings have been of this type.

Despite its name, this judicial proceeding does not involve an initial decision by the Court of Justice, followed by a decision of the national court. Rather, it is an interlocutory proceeding in the sense that the underlying case begins in the national court; and, after an interlocutory hearing before the Court of Justice in which the national judge seeks an interpretation of Community law relevant to his or her decision, it ends in the national court as well.

The Preliminary Ruling Proceeding is concerned solely with the question of Community law posed to it, and the Court of Justice reaches its decision without regard to the final decision in the underlying case. Applying the Court of Justice's ruling and the rendering of a final judgment in the case remain the province of the national court. It is important to emphasize that the Court of Justice has not been placed over the national courts and therefore is not empowered to reverse the judicial decisions of the national courts but only to provide them with helpful support.

The Court of Justice issues a preliminary ruling only upon the request of a national court. In order for a national court to make a request for such a ruling, it must find that a provision of Community law applicable to its case is in need of interpretation or that there is a justifiable doubt about the legality of the Community law provision under application. The national court must also determine that a decision on its legal question is necessary to its judgment in the pending case.

In its preliminary ruling, the Court of Justice resolves issues regarding the interpretation and validity of Community law or the validity of acts of the Community institutions. The Article 177 proceeding can thus be based on Community treaties (which according to the Court of Justice have direct applicability in the Member States) as well as on regulations, judicial decisions, and when certain conditions are met, on directives that have direct applicability in the Member States. In addition, understandings, declarations and resolutions of the Council of Ministers as well as legal acts of the European Parliament can be the subject of a Preliminary Ruling Proceeding.

One important purpose of this proceeding can be seen from the goals and mission of the Community as well as from the proceeding's effect, namely, the consistent development of Community law. To the extent that Community law is directly applicable in the Member States and therefore subject to the interpretation of their national courts, a danger of inconsistent application and interpretation exists. Such a danger runs afoul of the Community goal of integration. If the development of Community law were left solely to the national courts, they would tend to interpret the treaties, regulations, directives, etc., of the Community in light of their own nation's legal tradition and methods.

The Preliminary Ruling Proceeding provides a way of preventing the threatened inconsistent interpretations of Community law from nation to nation and instead fosters its standardization and even application throughout the Community. At the same time, the proceeding helps the judges of the various nations of the Community with the difficult tasks which may arise out of the co-existence of national and Community law.

The proceeding also provides a mechanism whereby the Court of Justice can „flesh out" the meaning of the often generally stated principles of the treaties. Both the Preliminary Ruling Proceeding of Article 177 as well as the Treaty Violation Proceeding of Article 169 involve the submission to the Court of Justice of cases whose resolution has significance and meaning for the entire Community. Both proceedings give the Court the opportunity of interpreting Community law in the context of concrete situations. The development of Community law into a self-contained and unified system is fostered by the Court's gradual development of the law on a case by case basis.

Only a "court of a Member State" can initiate a Preliminary Ruling Proceeding. The parties of the underlying case (for example, citizens and/or organizations who have a dispute with a government agency), the institutions of the Community, administrative agencies of the Member States as well as courts from countries who do not belong to the Community are not entitled to seek a preliminary ruling from the Court of Justice.

The term "court of a Member State" means an independent judicial tribunal which derives its power to resolve disputes from the public. Up to now, the Court of Justice has only heard requests for a preliminary ruling filed by national courts which have independent authority to resolve disputes and cases on their merits. Administrative tribunals which provide citizens or groups an opportunity to be heard or to protest but whose decision-makers lack the requisite independence are not considered to be a "court of the Member State" in this sense.

Despite the fact that only a court can initiate a Preliminary Ruling Proceeding, this proceeding still serves the important function of protecting the individual's Community law rights. As a result of the legal decisions of the Court of Justice providing for direct applicability and priority of Community law, citizens and/or groups can often assert their Community law rights in national court proceedings. These national courts in turn have the right to initiate a Preliminary Ruling Proceeding. In this way, the citizens' Community rights are indirectly protected; for example, parties to a proceeding before a national court can defend themselves against actions of a Member State which violate Community law by requesting that the court submit the question of the compatibility of the Member State's action (or lack of action) with provisions of Community law to the Court of Justice.

Citizens' protection is, as previously stated, indirect only as citizens cannot compel the national court to submit questions of Community law to the Court of Justice. The citizen or group can only attempt to persuade the national court of the necessity of instituting a Preliminary Ruling Procedure. If the national court believes that its case is not significantly impacted by Community law, it is not required to seek a preliminary ruling from the Court of Justice.

Chapter 11

ANTITRUST LAW IN THE EUROPEAN COMMUNITY

Bernd Tremml and Andreas Meisterernst

I. Introduction to the Antitrust Law of the European Community

Just as in the United States, in the European Community (EC) the freedom to do business is subject to many restrictions. The EC as well as the individual country members of the EC (Member States) may impose restrictions on trade on the basis of economic, environmental, safety and other grounds. From the perspective of a person engaged in business in the Common Market, the antitrust provisions of the Treaty Establishing the European Economic Community as amended (EEC Treaty), which generally encompasses Articles 85-90, and the regulations adopted pursuant to the Treaty, comprise on the one hand some of the most significant restrictions on the freedom to do business but on the other foster fair competition and the integration of markets on the other. The Commission of the European Community enforces these laws and is empowered to impose fines on businesses in the event of a violation.

In addition to the European antitrust laws, national antitrust laws exist in most Member States. The purpose of such laws is to control unfair competitive practices within the Member State's internal market. According to the decisions of the European Court of Justice, the European antitrust law takes precedence over national antitrust law. To the extent a Member State's law has cross-border effects, practices which are allowed under Articles 85-90 of the EEC Treaty may not be forbidden by a national legislature. Due to the fact that most contemporary business activities have an impact on more than one Member State, the national antitrust laws currently play a limited role and will therefore not be discussed.

II. Prohibitions contained in Articles 85-87 of the EEC Treaty

A. Article 85

Article 85 of the EEC Treaty states:

1. The following shall be prohibited as incompatible with the Common Market: all agreements between enterprises, decisions by associations of undertakings and concerted practices which may affect trade between Member States and which have as their object or effect the prevention, restriction or distortion of competition within the Common Market, and in particular those which:
   (a) directly or indirectly fix purchase or selling prices or any other trading conditions;
   (b) limit or control production, markets, technical development or investment;
   (c) share markets or sources of supply;
   (d) apply dissimilar conditions to equivalent transactions with other trading parties, thereby placing them at a competitive disadvantage;
   (e) make the conclusion of contracts subject to acceptance by the other parties of supplementary obligations which, by their nature or according to

commercial usage, have no connection with the subject of such contracts.

2. Any agreements or decisions prohibited pursuant to this article shall be automatically void.
3. The provisions of paragraph 1 may, however, be declared inapplicable in the case of:

- any agreement or category of agreements between undertakings;
- any decision or category of decision by associations of undertakings;
- any concerted practice or category of concerted practices which contributes to improving the production or distribution of goods or to promoting technical or economic progress while allowing consumers a fair share of the resulting benefit and which does not:
  (a) impose on the undertakings concerned restrictions which are not indispensable to the attainment of these objectives;
  (b) afford such undertaking the possibility of eliminating competition in respect of a substantial part of the products in question.

The purpose of Article 85 is not only to regulate competition but to integrate the national markets. Its provisions apply to "horizontal agreements" (agreements between competitors operating at the same level in the economic process) and to "vertical agreements" (agreements between non-competing enterprises operating at different levels). This means that the primary concern of the EC antitrust law is not, in contrast to US antitrust law, to assure interbrand competition.

An "agreement" in the sense of article 85 EEC Treaty is not just a formal contract. The provisions of Article 85 are always applicable when modes of behavior exist which have economic relevance such as informal agreements, imposed agreements and agreements declared to be non-binding. The provisions of Article 85, par. 1 enumerate several examples of forbidden cartels, such as discount cartels, price cartels, condition-fixing cartels, market-information agencies, tied distribution systems, prohibition of cross deliveries and agreements which discriminate against third persons.

A "concerted practice," as that term is used in Article 85, is even less formal than an agreement and difficult to differentiate from so-called "parallel behavior". The European Court of Justice declared in "ICI vs. Commission" (Case 48/69):

> Although parallel behavior may not by itself be identified with a concerted practice, it may however amount to strong evidence of such a practice if it leads to conditions of competition which do not correspond to the normal condition of the market, having regard to the nature of the products, the size and number of the enterprises and the volume of the said market.

The relevant market is not necessarily the entire market but only that portion of the Common Market which can be viewed as an independent business area in which competitive relationships can be affected or destroyed. Although Article 85 is primarily intended to apply to deals which affect trade between Member States, it can also apply to internal deals made in one Member State and to deals made between parties located outside of the EC. In "Ahlström Osakyhtio vs. Commission" (1988) ECR 5193, the Court of Justice of the European Community declared:

> It should be noted that the main sources of supply of wood pulp are outside the Community in Canada, the United States, Sweden and Finland and that the market therefore has global dimensions. Where wood pulp producers established in those countries sell directly to purchasers established in the Community and engage in price competition in order to win orders from those customers, that constitutes competition within the Common Market.
>
> It follows that where those producers concert on the prices to be charged to their customers in the Community and put that concertation into effect by selling at prices which are actually coordinated, they are taking part in concertation which has the object and effect of restricting competition within the Common Market within the meaning of Article 85 of the Treaty.

"Restraint of competition" has not been defined abstractly or generally by the Court of Justice of the European Community. Every case must be analyzed individually under the criterion of what possibilities enterprises would have on the open market if the suspect agreement did not exist. The restrictive impact of the agreement or concerted practice on competition must be significant. Administrative provisions exist which define the circumstances under which the Commission will view the restrictive effect of an agreement on competition to be insignificant [Commission Notice on Agreements of Minor Importance (1986) OJ C231/2)]. These provisions appear in the check list for minor cases contained in III. F. below.

B. Articles 86 and 87

Article 86 of the EEC Treaty forbids an enterprise from using its market- controlling position to dictate prices or to drive out competitor enterprises. An enterprise has a controlling market position if it is in a position to avoid participation in competition or to hinder competition on certain cross-border markets for comparable products. For example, a controlling market position is present if a business is able to control the raw-materials market or business channels.

In any case, the most important indicator that an enterprise has a controlling market position is control of a share of the market which significantly exceeds the share of its competitors. A controlling market position is presumed if the enterprise's market share exceeds 50%.

In order to establish a violation of Article 86, however, it is not enough to show that an enterprise has a controlling market position. Rather, it must also be shown that the enterprise has misused its market controlling position; for example, that it has forced an inappropriate price or business condition on a competitor.

Article 87 of the EEC Treaty requires prior EC Commission authorization for mergers which have Community-wide impact.

III. Exemptions to European Antitrust laws

A. Introduction

The practices prohibited by European antitrust law are broadly enough defined to encompass many forms of business relationships which are often desirable from an economic standpoint. Such business relationships include patent agreements, license agreements, know-how agreements and exclusive distribution or purchase agreements. In order to deal with these types of special cases, the Commission is empowered under Article 85 (3) of the EEC Treaty to provide for exceptions to the antitrust prohibitions. The Commission exercises this power through the granting of exemptions on a case-by-case basis as well as through the adoption of regulations granting categorical exemptions known as "block exemptions."

B. Block exemptions

The Commission has already issued several regulations under Article 85 (3) which define the criteria for determining certain categories of agreements which are exempt from the European antitrust law. The most important regulations and the corresponding agreements addressed in these regulations are:

- Commission Regulation 1983/83 (exclusive distribution agreements)
- Commission Regulation 1984/83 (exclusive purchasing agreements)
- Commission Regulation 417/85 (specialization agreements) as amended by Commission Regulation 151/93
- Commission Regulation 418/85 (research and development agreements)
- Commission Regulation 2349/84 (patent-licensing agreements) as amended by Commission Regulation 151/93
- Commission Regulation 4087/88 (franchise agreements)
- Commission Regulation 556/89 (know-how licensing agreements) as amended by Commission Regulation 151/93
- Commission Regulation regarding contracts for the transfer of technology, which came into effect on April 4, 1996. This regulation removes computer software and hardware contracts from the coverage

of block exemptions No. 2349/84 regarding patent licensing agreements and No. 556/89 regarding know-how agreements

The structure of the various block exemption regulations is very similar. Typically, Article 1 of such a regulation declares that the agreements defined in it are exempt from the provisions of Article 85 (1) of the EEC Treaty. Article 2 typically sets forth additional permissible contract clauses (the so-called "white list"). Article 3 usually contains a list of terms which, when contained in the agreements defined in Article 1, result in the agreement losing its exemption (these terms have come to be known as the "black list"). The remaining articles contain administrative provisions, extend or restrict the scope of Article 2 and 3 and provide additional definitions.

As a rule, the block exemption regulations are so detailed that it is possible to determine exactly what type of contracts are exempted from Article 85 (1) of the EEC Treaty. According to some critics, the extensive detail in the regulations has led to the use of standard types of agreements and a lack of innovation on the part of enterprises in the development of new contracts.

Qualifying for a block exemption requires no application to or formal authorization from the EC Commission. If an agreement meets the requirements of a particular block exemption regulation, then it is simply exempt from the EC antitrust laws.

C. Example of a block exemption regulation: Commission Regulation 2349/84 pertaining to patent-licensing agreements

Because patent licensing agreements are of special economic interest, this section contains a short overview of the most important provisions of the block exemption regulation pertaining to them (Commission Regulation 2349/84).

According to Article 1 of the regulation, Article 85(1) of the EEC Treaty shall not apply to: (1) patent licensing agreements, (2) agreements combining the licensing of patents and the communication of know-how and (3) agreements combining the licensing of patent to agreements regarding trademarks, to which only two enterprises are party and which include one or more of the following obligations:

- an obligation on the licensor not to grant other enterprises a license to exploit the licensed invention,
- an obligation on the licensor not to exploit the licensed invention himself in the situation where the licensee manufactures the product himself or has it manufactured by a connecting enterprise or subcontractor,
- an obligation on the licensee not to exploit the licensed invention in territories which are reserved to the licensor in the situation where the licensee manufactures the product himself or has it manufactured by a connecting enterprise or subcontractor,
- an obligation not to make use of the licensed invention in territories which are licensed to other licensees,
- an obligation not to pursue an active policy of putting the licensed product on the market in territories which are licensed to other licensees,
- an obligation not to put the licensed product on the market in territories which are licensed to other licensees for a period up to five years measured from the date when the product is first put on the

market. (Note: Like several of the above mentioned obligations, this obligation is only permissible in the situation in which the licensee manufactures the product himself or has it manufactured by a connecting enterprise or subcontractor),

- an obligation to use only the licensor's trademark or get up determined by the licensor to distinguish the licensed product.

Contractual terms which are of the same nature as the above mentioned but which are more limited in scope, are also permitted. According to Article 2, the following obligations imposed on the licensee, known as the "white list," are allowed:

- an obligation to procure goods or services from the licensor if such obligation is necessary from a technical standpoint,
- an obligation to pay a minimum royalty or to produce a minimum quantity,
- an obligation to restrict the exploitation to one or more fields of use,
- an obligation not to exploit the patent after termination of the agreement in so far as the patent is still in force,
- an obligation not to sublicense,
- an obligation to mark the licensed product with an indication of the patentee's name, the patent or the agreement,
- an obligation not to divulge know-how,
- obligations to assist the licensor in actions against infringements of the patent without prejudice to the licensee's right to challenge the validity of the patent,
- an obligation to observe specifications concerning the minimum quality of the licensed product.

Article 2 allows an obligation on the parties to communicate to one another any experience gained in exploiting the licensed inventions and to grant one another a license in respect of inventions relating to improvements and new applications, provided that such communication or license is non-exclusive. Finally, Article 2 provides that an obligation imposed on the licensor to grant the licensee more favorable terms than those granted to others is permissible.

According to Article 3, Article 85 (1) of the EEC Treaty shall nevertheless apply to the agreements defined in Article 1 if such agreements contain one of the following terms (the so-called "black list"):

- the licensee is prohibited from challenging the validity of licensed patents,
- the duration of the agreement is automatically extended beyond the expiration of the existing patents unless the agreement grants each party the right to terminate the contract at least annually after expiration,
- one party is restricted from competing with the other party in a way which is not expressly allowed in Article 1; (an obligation on licensees to use their best endeavors to exploit the invention, however, is permissible),
- the licensee is charged royalties on products which are not patented or for the use of know-how which has entered the public domain (permissible, however, is an agreement, in order to facilitate payment, that the royalty payments for the use of a licensed invention shall be spread over a period extending beyond the life of the licensed patents or the entry of the know-how into public domain),
- the quantity of licensed products is subject to limitations,

- one party is restricted in the determination of prices,
- one party is restricted as to which customers may be served within the licensed territory unless such restriction is allowed by Article 1,
- the licensee is obliged to assign the licensor rights in or to patents for improvements or for new applications,
- the licensee is induced at the time of the signing of the agreement to accept further licenses, goods or services which he or she does not want unless these are necessary for a satisfactory exploitation of the licensed invention from a technical standpoint,
- the licensee is restricted for a period of more than five years from putting the product on the market in territories licensed to other licensees within the Common Market; or, does not do so as a result of a concerted practice between the parties,
- one or both of the parties are required to

(1) refuse, without an objective reason to meet the demand from users or resellers who would market products in other territories within the Common Market

- or -

(2) make it difficult for users or resellers to obtain the products from others; or one or both of the parties engage in the conduct set forth in (1) or (2) due to a concerted practice between the parties.

Article 4 of the Regulation contains administrative provisions. According to Article 5, the regulation shall not apply to the following:

- agreements between members of a patent pool which relate to the pooled patents,
- patent-licensing agreements between competitors who hold interests in a joint venture or between one

of them and the joint venture if the licensing agreements relate to the activities of the joint venture

- agreements under which the parties, albeit in separate agreements or through connected enterprises, grant each other reciprocal patent or trade-mark licenses or reciprocal sales rights for unprotected products or exchange know-how (Note: This exclusion from the regulation only applies where the parties are: (1) competitors in relation to the products covered by those agreements and (2) subject to territorial restrictions within the Common Market on the manufacture, use or putting on the market of the products covered by these agreements or on the use of the licensed processes.),
- licensing agreements in respect of plant breeders' rights.

Articles 6 to 14 provide definitions and additional administrative provisions.

D. Negative Clearances

In the event that an enterprise is uncertain whether a project or transaction contains a competitive practice prohibited by the European antitrust law, it may apply for a negative clearance, or certification by the Commission that a specific project or transaction contains no practice which violates European antitrust law. The Commission will not provide a negative clearance, however, if a block exemption is clearly applicable to the intended contract. If the conditions for a negative clearance are not present, the Commission will treat the application as an application for an individual exemption.

E. Individual exemptions

The EC Commission may exempt, upon application by an enterprise, certain contracts or transactions from the application of Article 85 (1) of the EEC Treaty. An enterprise is entitled to apply for an individual exemption if the agreement, transaction or practice in question falls within article 85 (1) and is not allowed by a block exemption.

Often an individual exemption is sought when the contract is clearly prohibited by a block exemption regulation. In such cases, the application will be granted by the Commission only if the parties are able to submit valid arguments why, in light of the individual circumstances of the applicant, a deviation from the generalized provisions of the regulation is warranted.

Article 85 (3) contains four conditions which must be met in order to receive an individual exemption. The applicant must show that the agreement, transaction or practice:

(1) will improve the production of goods or promote economic progress,

(2) will result in the customers reaping a fair share of the agreement's, practice's or transaction's benefit,

(3) is free of unnecessary restraints

- and -

(4) does not eliminate competition.

In practice, an individual exemption will seldom be denied when only one condition has not been met.

Commission Decision 376/17 (Carbon Gas) provides an example of the application of these conditions in an individual exemption proceeding. In that case, the German branch of BP, in conjunction with a couple of other enterprises founded a company for the development and commercial exploitation of a new coal gasification procedure. The Commission granted an individual exemption under Article 85(3) ETC on the grounds that the agreement would: (1) lead to a significant reduction of costs, (2) lead to a stable supply to the consumers, (3) consisted of contractual terms which were all necessary in light of the aim of the agreement and (4) did not eliminate competition because various other competitive enterprises were involved in developing and testing similar procedures.

The exemption will not be granted if the Commission determines that it will lead to a monopoly position of the enterprises concerned. For this reason, the Commission often conditions the granting of the exemption on the applicant's fulfillment of enumerated steps designed to protect competition.

An exemption is always granted for a definite time period. Important administrative provisions relating to the exemption proceeding are contained in Council Regulation 17, as amended by the Accession Treaties and Regulations 59,118/63 and 2822/71. In addition, provisions for special administrative procedures are found in Article 3 of the Patent Licensing Regulation, Article 3 of the Know-how Licensing Regulation and Article 6 of the Research and Development Regulation. Under these regulations, the demand for exemption of certain contracts is deemed to be approved if the Commission does not deny the application within 6 months.

F. Minor cases

Agreements, decisions by associations or enterprises and concerted practices which fall within the provisions of the "Commission Notice on Agreements of Minor Importance" [(1986) OJ C231/2] require no exemption. The

Commission will not provide a negative clearance in these cases. If, due to exceptional circumstances, an agreement covered by this Notice nevertheless constitutes an antitrust violation under Article 85(1) of the EEC Treaty, the Commission will not impose fines.

Checklist for minor cases

a) Is there an agreement between enterprises?

Participating enterprises are defined as:

- the parties to the agreement

  - or -

- enterprises in which a party

  1. owns directly or indirectly more than half the capital or business assets

     - or -

  2. has the power to exercise more than half the voting rights

     - or -

  3. has the power to appoint more than 50% of the members of bodies which legally represent the company

     - or -

  4. has the right to manage the company's affairs

     - and -

- enterprises which directly or indirectly exercise the power(s) set forth in 1-4 above over a party to the agreement.

b) Are the enterprises engaged in the production or distribution of goods?

c) Are goods or services the subject of the agreement?

d) Do the participating enterprises offer other goods or services which are viewed by the customers to be equivalent in view of their characteristics, price and intended use?

e) Do the goods and services set forth in (c) together with the goods and services set forth in (d) represent 5 % or less of the total market?

In order to calculate the market share, it is necessary to determine the relevant product market and the relevant geographical market. The relevant product market includes, in addition to the contract goods and services, any other products which are identical or equivalent to them. The products must be interchangeable from the vantage point of the customer. If the contract products comprise a significant component of another product of the participating enterprises, then reference must be made to the latter product. The relevant geographical market is the area within the Community which is affected by the agreement. That market will often be narrower than the whole Common Market, where products are only bought and sold in limited quantities in certain areas or where the nature or characteristics of the products restrict their mobility; for instance, high transport costs.

f) Is the aggregate annual turnover of the participating enterprises equal to or less than 200 million ECU (at the moment about 160 million U.S. dollars)?

Aggregate turnover includes the turnover in all goods and services achieved during the last financial year by the participating enterprises, excluding taxes, and turnover generated between participating enterprises.

Where each of the questions above may be answered in the affirmative, the case in point will be deemed to be a "minor case." Moreover, even if the answer to (e) and/or (f) is *no*, a "minor case" is still shown if the aforementioned market share and/or turnover was, during the last two successive financial years, not exceeded by more than one-tenth.

IV. Sanctions and Judicial Review

Agreements not complying with the EC antitrust law are void, and the EC Commission as well as national antitrust authorities may impose severe penalties of up to forty million U.S. dollars for such violations.

Decisions of the Commission, e.g. the refusal to grant an individual exemption or a negative-clearance certification, as well as decisions of the national authorities can be challenged by the affected enterprises or persons. Suits may be filed by affected parties against individual decisions made by EC institutions as well as against EC regulations. Such suits must be filed in the EC Court of First Instance and instituted within two months of the notification of a decision to a party (in the case of an individual decision) or within two months of the publication of a new regulation.

All appeals based on errors of law alleged to have been made by the European Court of First Instance must be filed with the European Court of Justice. The European Court of Justice does not review factual matters.

Actions of the national authorities may be appealed only in the national courts in accordance with the Member State's law. This is true even if the challenged action exclusively concerns EC law.

If bodies of the EC cause damage to an enterprise or person by illegal acts, compensation from the European Community is also possible. Such claims must be filed in the European Court of First Instance, and in the event the claim is denied, an appeal to the European Court of Justice is available.

Chapter 12

UNFAIR TERMS IN CONSUMER CONTRACTS IN THE EUROPEAN COMMUNITY

Bernd Tremml and Andreas Meisterernst

I. Introduction

In light of a European market which is based on ever increasing numbers and types of products and services as well as standardization in the methods used in the marketing and sales of such products and services, protection for the consumer is more important than ever. Today's consumer is often neither able to understand the terms and conditions used in consumer contracts nor to appreciate the impact of these terms. Until recently, this problem was aggravated by the fact that the laws applicable to the sale of goods and services to consumers varied extensively throughout Europe -- a situation which frequently left European consumers completely in the dark when they purchased a good or service in a foreign country.

For these reasons, among others, the European Community enacted a law in 1993 designed to protect consumers. This law, which is in the form of a directive, is entitled: "Council Directive 93/13/ EEC of 5 April 1993 on Unfair Terms in Consumer Contracts." Directive 93/13 lays down, for the first time, standard consumer-protection rules to be followed throughout the European Community.

European law makes a distinction between directives and regulations. According to Art. 189, paragraph 2 of the EC Treaty, regulations have general applicability. They are binding in their entirety and directly applicable in all the countries which are members of the European Community (Member States). This means that regulations, depending on their content, can have a direct impact on the rights and duties of citizens and businesses. Directives, on the other hand, are only directly binding on the Member States to which they are addressed. According to Art. 189, paragraph 3 of the EC Treaty, directives are binding on the Member States as to the result to be achieved but leave to the national authorities the choice of how to achieve this result. In other words, the legislative branch of each of the Member States must incorporate the provisions of a directive into national law and, in so doing, may use the form and methods it sees fit. Usually, directives contain a certain date by which each Member State must have accomplished this incorporation.

Directives, therefore, in contrast to regulations, have no direct impact on businesses and citizens; they are neither designed to grant rights nor impose duties on private natural or legal persons. In the language of the European Court of Justice, directives have a vertical as opposed to a horizontal effect. This means that citizens or businesses involved in a dispute regarding rights which are the subject matter of a directive must look to their own national law and not the directive for relief. Therefore, "Directive 93/13/EWG of the Council of Ministers dated April 5, 1993 pertaining to Unfair Terms in Consumer Contracts" cannot be directly applied to the private citizens and businesses of the European Community but does, however, describe the common standards which the Member States must incorporate in their own consumer protection laws.

II. Directive 93/13 Pertaining to Unfair Terms in Consumer Contracts

A. Overview

The goal of Directive 93/13 is to ensure that a minimum level of consumer protection exists in the Member States of the European Community. This directive has the dual effects of encouraging the Member States to protect their consumers while at the same time making it easier, through the standardization of consumer protection laws, for businesses to sell their goods and services throughout the Community. Competition is thus encouraged and at least some of the distortions which result when products and services are marketed in countries under widely divergent conditions and laws are eliminated.

Accordingly, Article 1 of Directive 93/13 states that the directive's purpose is to encourage uniformity of the laws, regulations and administrative provisions of the Member States relating to unfair terms in contracts between a seller or supplier and a consumer. Because the adoption or retention by Member States of more stringent consumer-protection laws is specifically allowed by Art. 8, it follows that the retention or adoption of a lesser level of protection than that set forth in the directive is not.

Member States were given until December 31, 1994 to bring into force the laws, regulations and administrative provisions necessary to comply with Directive 93/13. For this reason, Article 10 (2) states that the provisions of the directive shall first be applicable to consumer contracts entered into after December 31, 1994.

B. Scope

The provisions of Directive 93/13 apply to the terms of contracts between consumers and sellers or suppliers of goods and services. A consumer is defined in Article 2 (c) as any natural person who enters into the type of contract covered by the directive for purposes which are not related to trade, business or profession. Under this definition, it is not the subjective intention of the buyer of goods and services but rather objective circumstances which are capable of being perceived by the seller or supplier that determine his or her status as a consumer. If the buyer of goods or services is also in business, then all sales contracts which have an objective relationship with the buyer's business are not consumer transactions. If the goods or services sold are used both in the buyer's private as well as business dealings, then the buyer's customer status depends on which use predominates.

Article 2 (c) defines a seller or supplier as a natural or legal person who enters into the types of contracts covered by the directive for the purpose of his or her private or publicly owned trade, business or profession. German law would add that a seller or supplier is one who engages in sales or service for the purposes of making a profit.

According to Article 4, contracts for the sale of goods and services as well as for the use of such goods are covered by the directive. Rental contracts thus fall under the directive's coverage.

Service contracts are defined in the directive as the provision of services through any form; for example, through work or service contracts, travel or vacation contracts, financial services contracts (including loan and insurance contracts), etc.

Because the individual Member States are the ones who, through appropriate legislation, bring the Directive's provisions to life, the laws which the States accordingly enact are of national, not international, impact. Nevertheless, Art. 6 (2) requires Member States to take all necessary measures within their powers to ensure that their citizens' consumer rights are not lost through choice-of-law contractual terms which opt for the applicability of a non-Member State's law. If, for example, the laws of countries outside the European Community could be consistently chosen to apply to contracts with European consumers and these third countries provided fewer consumer rights than provided in the European Community, the purposes of the directive would be defeated. Art. 6 assumes that the Member States have jurisdiction to regulate conflict-of-law contractual clauses in situation s in which the consumer contract has a close connection to the Member State.

C. Exclusions

Excluded from Directive 93/13 are contractual terms which either reflect mandatory statutory or regulatory provisions or the provisions or principles of international conventions to which the Member States or the Community are a party [Article 1 (2)]. This exclusion ensures that terms which a Member State's law requires to be included in a consumer contract or terms which have been otherwise included as a result of that law are not subject to scrutiny under the directive.

In addition, according to paragraph 10 of the directive's preamble, contracts relating to employment, succession rights, rights under family law and to the incorporation and organization of companies as well as partnership agreements are excluded from the directive's coverage.

Further, terms in a consumer contract which describe the main subject matter of the contract or the quality/price ratio of the goods or services supplied are also excluded from coverage. This latter exclusion is necessary to ensure that the directive is not seen or used as a price-control law.

D. Exclusions based on individually negotiated terms

Perhaps the most significant exclusion from Directive 93/13's coverage are terms which have been individually negotiated by the consumer and seller or supplier. The directive designates such terms "individual terms." Individual terms are not affirmatively defined in the directive; instead, they are defined indirectly by stating when an individual term is not present. According to Article 3 (2), a contractual term which has been previously drafted by the seller or supplier, thus providing no real opportunity for a consumer to influence its content, is not an individual term. In particular, terms contained in pre-formulated standard-form contracts are not individual terms.

The German case law holds that even if a consumer has been thoroughly informed about the meaning and impact of a term, this fact does not transform a pre-formulated term into an individual term. Irrelevant as well under German law, is a signed declaration by the customer to the effect that the contract's terms have been individually negotiated. By the same token, the fact that a standard form contract specifically solicits changes or deletions by the consumer or contains blanks for the customer to fill in, does not transform these terms into individual ones.

Much more relevant in determining whether a term in an otherwise standard form contract is an individual term, is the examination of whether the seller or supplier was, as a matter of fact, ready and prepared to negotiate over the term. The seller's amenability to negotiation must clearly and sincerely be expressed to the consumer. The consumer, in short, must possess the real possibility to influence the contractual term. It is irrelevant that the businessperson's notary, attorney or other representative has drafted the term. Clearly, such a third party has an interest in strengthening or establishing a business relationship with the businessperson.

According to Article 3 (2) sentence two, the fact that one specific term or certain aspects of a term have been individually negotiated does not mean that the directive is inapplicable to the remaining terms if an overall assessment of the contract indicates that it is nevertheless a pre-formulated standard form contract. Thus, a situation can arise in which certain terms in a contract are subject to the directive's scrutiny, whereas other individual terms are not.

In a pre-formulated standard form contract, the seller or supplier has the burden of proving that one or more of its terms are individual terms. In non-standard form contracts, the burden of proof lies with the consumer to show that a term was not individually negotiated.

E. General definition of an unfair term

Article 3 (1) defines a term as unfair if, contrary to the requirements of good faith, it causes a significant imbalance in the parties' rights and obligations arising under the contract to the detriment of the consumer. The phrase "a significant imbalance" is indefinite and in need of interpretation. Important interpretive sources are the laws passed by the Member States in response to Directive 93/13 and the subsequent interpretation of these laws by the national courts.

Here it should be pointed out that the Member States' interpretations of Directive 93/13 are useful only to the extent that such interpretations are based on the purpose and intent of the institutions of the European Community that enacted this law. In other words, Member States have a duty to interpret Community law independently of their own national law. Meeting this duty (which, in the legal language of European law, is known as the duty to "autonomously interpret directives") is one of the fundamental keys to the ultimate success of the goal of Directive 93/13 to unify consumer-protection laws throughout the Community.

A German law entitled "Law for the Regulation of Standard Business Terms" ["Gesetz zur Regelung der Allgemeinen Geschäftsbedingungen" (AGBG)], is the law chosen by Germany as the vehicle for incorporating Directive 93/13 into its national law. The AGBG interprets a significant imbalance as one which is present when a particular term is at odds with the essential principles of the consumer-protection laws or when the result of a particular term is to restrict the essential rights or contractual obligations to such an extent that the purpose or goal of the contract is in danger of not being met. Whether a term is unfair under German law must be determined by considering both the individual interests of the parties and the standard practices in the particular trade or industry. The term should be assessed in light of the subject matter, purpose and particular features of the contract involved. Its fairness must be judged in light of the contract as a whole. A significant imbalance can especially be said to be present when the consumer, as a result of the term or terms, is unreasonably disadvantaged.

According to Article 4 (1) of the directive, an assessment of the unfairness of a contractual term must take into account the nature of the goods or services supplied in the contract, other terms in the contract at issue or in any other contract upon which the contract is dependent as well as all circumstances present at the time the parties entered into the contract. Two of these circumstances which paragraph 16 of the preamble particularly stresses are the respective bargaining positions of the parties and whether or not the consumer has been induced to agree to the challenged term or terms.

Thus, Directive 93/13 contemplates an examination of a challenged term at two levels. First, one must look at the term without considering the situation of the parties in order to determine if, from a generalized, objective perspective, the term itself is unfair. Second, the term's fairness must be assessed in light of the individual case. In this second step, it is important to determine if the circumstances surrounding the entering into of the contract provide any reason to suspect that the term is unfair. In particular, one should consider whether a consumer has been exploited due to the seller or supplier's intellectual superiority in business matters or greater business experience as well as whether there is any evidence of unconscionable behavior or over-reaching on the part of the seller or supplier.

According to Article 5, the terms contained in written contracts must be drafted in plain and intelligible language. Where there is doubt about the meaning of a term, the interpretation which is most favorable to the consumer will prevail.

Exactly what constitutes an unfair term under Article 3 of Directive 93/13 is further illuminated by its appendix. The directive's appendix contains a representative list of terms which may be regarded as unfair. Unlike the provisions in the articles of the directive itself, the terms contained in its appendix are intended only to provide guidelines for the Member States; the directive does not mandate that such terms be designated as unfair in the Member State's incorporating legislation [Article 3 (3)]. Nevertheless, it can be assumed that these terms have to a large extent been designated in the Member States' national law incorporating Directive 93/13 as unfair and that the prohibition of such terms now forms the foundation of European consumer-protection law. For this reason, each of the terms contained in the appendix of Directive 93/13 are discussed below.

Following an examination of the appendix's terms, a short explanation of the corresponding German law is given. The explanation is provided to illustrate how a Member State typically incorporates the non-mandatory provisions of Directive 93/13's appendix into its own national law. It should not be overlooked, however, that because the directive's appendix is not binding on the Member States, there may be variations between the terms deemed unfair in the appendix and terms deemed unfair under national law. This variation in the content of the directive and the national law is not possible in the case of the mandatory articles of Directive 93/13.

F. Representative list of unfair terms

Number 1 (a) of the appendix designates such terms as unfair that have the object or effect of excluding or limiting the legal liability of a seller or supplier in the event of the consumer's personal injury or death resulting from an act or omission of the seller or supplier. Germany's "Law for the

Regulation of Standard Business Terms," which, as indicated above, is the national law incorporating Directive 93/13, does not contain a provision with the exact same meaning. Instead, German law renders all such terms unenforceable that exclude liability resulting from gross negligence.

Number 1 (b) designates terms which have the object or effect of inappropriately excluding or limiting the legal rights of consumers in their relationships with the seller or supplier or another party in the event of the seller's or supplier's total or partial non-performance or inadequate performance of any of the contractual obligations as unfair. Germany's law provides in AGBG par. 11 (2),(3),(8),(9), that consumer rights provided by German law may not be inappropriately excluded or limited in the consumer contract. In particular, contractual terms which limit the consumer's ability to terminate the contract or seek damages in the event of partial or total breach by the seller are unenforceable. Moreover, German law designates contractual terms unfair that prohibit the consumer from withholding performance until the seller has performed.

Number 1 (c) designates terms unfair that have the object or effect of making an agreement binding on the consumer while the seller or supplier's own performance is subject to a condition whose realization depends on his discretion. Such a provision, while not specifically prohibited in German law, would most likely be deemed unenforceable under the general provisions of par. 9 of the AGBG. That paragraph is similar to Article 3 of the directive and designates terms which unreasonably disadvantage the consumer as unfair.

Under Number 1 (d), terms are unfair which have the object or effect of permitting the seller or supplier to retain sums paid by the consumer where the latter decides not to conclude or perform the contract, without providing a reciprocal right to the consumer in the event the seller or supplier is the party who cancels the contract. The corresponding German provision renders void contractual terms which allow the seller or supplier, in the event the customer exercises a legal option not to fulfill the contract or otherwise terminates the contract, to withhold an unreasonable sum for the consumer's use of any property or goods, services or rights provided the consumer or as remuneration for expenses incurred by the seller or supplier (par. 10, sec. 7 AGBG).

Any term which has the object or effect of requiring consumers who fail to fulfill their obligations to pay a disproportionately high sum in compensation is unfair according to Number 1 (e) of the appendix. Par. 11 (6) of the AGBG extends this consumer protection by prohibiting all contract penalties, regardless of their amount, which the seller or supplier seeks to impose in the event that the consumer fails or delays in accepting performance, delays or fails to pay or backs out of a contract altogether.

Number 1 (f) and (g) deem terms unfair that give the seller or supplier discretion to terminate the contract without providing the consumer the same privilege. Unfair as well are terms which allow a seller or supplier who terminates a contract to retain sums paid by the consumer for a performance which has yet to be delivered. Finally, in the absence of serious grounds, it is unfair for the seller or supplier to terminate a contract of indeterminate duration without reasonable notice. Par. 10 (3) of the AGBG has incorporated this latter provision into German law: any contractual provision in a standard form contract which gives the seller or supplier the right to refuse performance without a factually justifiable reason is unfair.

Under Number 1 (h), a term whose object or effect is to automatically extend a contract of fixed duration absent affirmative objection by the consumer is unfair if the consumer is required to express his objection unreasonably early. The corresponding provision of German law is found in par. 11 (12) AGBG, which provides that in contracts providing for the regular delivery of goods or services, any terms which provide for a contract duration of more than two years are void. Any automatic extension provisions are limited to one year at a time, and the customer cannot be required to express a desire to cancel the contract more than three months before the expiration of the initial contract or its extension.

Number 1 (i) states that terms which have the object or effect of irrevocably binding customers to terms they had no real opportunity of becoming acquainted with before entering into the contract are unfair. For example, such an unfair term could be a provision in the contract that the consumer has read and understands all the terms of the contract. Under German law, a contractual provision such as this in a standard form contract would also be unenforceable because it has the effect of altering the amount of proof consumers must present regarding their understanding of the contract's terms. Such a provision therefore violates par. 11 (15) of the AGBG, which deems as void any terms whose effect are to alter the burden of proof to the disadvantage of a party through the use of a contractual confirmation.

Number 1 (j), (k), (l), and (m) render unfair all terms granting the seller or supplier the right to unilaterally alter the terms in a contract without having a valid reason which is specified in the contract. Such unfair unilateral changes include, in particular, changes without a valid reason to the characteristics of the product or service to be provided. Moreover, contractual terms which provide that the seller or supplier at the time of delivery may first determine the price or increase the price are unfair unless the consumer is given the right to cancel the contract if the final price is too high in relation to the price agreed to at the time the contract was entered into. Finally, giving the seller or supplier the right to determine whether the goods or services supplied are in conformity with the contract or the exclusive right to interpret any term in the contract is deemed unfair by the directive. German law has incorporated certain aspects of these proposed prohibitions. Under par. 11 (1) AGBG, a term which allows the seller to increase the contract price within four months of the date when the contract was entered into is unenforceable. According to par. 10 (4) AGBG, a term in a standard form contract which allows the seller or supplier to alter their performance is invalid when, even in light of the interests of the seller or supplier, it is unreasonable to expect the consumer to concede to such a unilateral change.

Number 1 (n) designates unfair any contractual terms that have the object or effect of limiting the seller's or supplier's obligation to respect the commitments of their agents or which provide that an agent's commitments are not binding on the principal unless a particular formality is present. This issue is not specifically addressed in the AGBG, but principals are generally responsible for their agent's actions under German law.

According to Number 1 (o), terms whose object or effect are to oblige consumers to fulfill all of their obligations even when the seller or supplier does not do so are unfair.

Germany's corresponding provision is contained in par. 11 (2) of the AGBG, which provides that contractual terms which prevent or limit the right of the consumer to withhold performance until the seller or supplier has performed are unenforceable.

Number 1 (p) deems a contractual provision to be unfair when it allows the seller or supplier to transfer their rights and obligations under the contract without first obtaining the consumer's special consent and when the transfer could increase the consumer's risk. Par. 11 (13) of the AGBG provides similarly that a standard form contract which allows the seller or supplier to unilaterally transfer their rights or responsibilities to a third party is unfair unless this third party is specifically named in the contract and/or the consumer is given the option of terminating the contract rather than accepting the transfer.

Terms whose object or effect are to exclude or hinder a consumer's right to take legal action or exercise any other legal remedy are unfair according to Number 1 (q). Especially included in this suspect category are terms which require the consumer to take disputes exclusively to an arbitration panel which is not covered by legal provisions, unduly restricting the evidence available to a consumer or imposing on a consumer a burden of proof which, according to law, should lie with the other party. One of these provisions of Number 1 (q) is found specifically in German law. According to par. 11 (15) AGBG, a contractual term in a standard form contract whereby the seller or supplier alters the burden of proof to the disadvantage of the consumer is unfair. Moreover, the directive's suggested provision pertaining to terms which restrict the consumer's right to take legal action would be deemed adverse to the general provision of the AGBG contained in par. 9.

Number 2 of the appendix carves out certain exceptions for the providers of financial services. For example, financial service providers are excluded from No. 1 (g). As a result, a contractual term reserving to the suppliers of financial services the right to unilaterally terminate a contract of indeterminate duration without notice where there is a valid reason is not unfair. No. 2 also sanctions contractual terms which permit the supplier of financial services to alter the rate of interest payable by the consumer or to increase the amount of other financial service charges without notice as long as there is a valid reason for it, the consumer is notified of the change at the earliest possible opportunity and the consumer has the right to terminate the contract based on such change.

Number 1 (g), (j), and (l) b of the appendix do not, according to Number 2 (c), apply to the following transactions: transactions in transferable securities, financial instruments and other products or services whose price is linked to fluctuations in a stock-exchange quotation or index or a financial market rate that the seller or supplier does not control. These same exemptions are afforded contracts for the purchase or sale of foreign currency, traveler's checks or international money orders denominated in foreign currency.

G. Impact of unfair terms on the enforcement of the contract

Article 6 (1) requires the Member States to include in their own national laws a provision that unfair terms used in a contract between a consumer and a seller or supplier shall not be binding and that the contract shall continue to bind the parties only if it is capable of continuing in existence without the unfair terms. This provision corresponds to par. 6 of the AGBG. According to this paragraph, if contractual terms are declared void, they will be replaced with the pertinent term provided by law. One effect of that is to render void the so-called "rescue clause." A rescue clause typically provides that in the event that a term is declared void, it shall be replaced with a term which, to the greatest extent legally possible, results in the same effect as the unenforceable term. Such rescue clauses are no longer valid in standard form contracts because of the German law mandate that it is the legal term and not a term which most closely approximates the unfair term which must be inserted into the contract.

In addition, German law also clarifies the circumstances under which the contract as a whole will continue to be enforceable despite the unfair term or terms. Par. 6, sec. 3 of the AGBG provides that the entire contract is void if continuing the contract with the new legal term would result in an undue hardship to one of the parties. Such an undue hardship is present only in the situation in which enforcement of the contract would lead to a severe imbalance in the value of the consideration paid by the parties.

H. Methods of enforcing consumer rights

Member States are required by Article 7 (1) to ensure that adequate and effective means exist to prevent the continued use of unfair terms in contracts between consumers and sellers or suppliers. Article 7 (2) states that those means shall include provisions whereby persons or organizations having a legitimate interest under national law in protecting consumers may seek a ruling from national courts or other administrative bodies regarding whether certain contractual terms drawn up for general use are unfair. Such a legal action may be directed at a single seller or supplier, at a group of sellers or suppliers from the same economic sector or at seller or supplier associations which use or recommend use of the challenged term. [Article 7 (3)]. A corresponding rule is found in German law in par. 13 of the AGBG.

III. Conclusion

This chapter has provided an overview of the consumer-protection law in the European Community pertaining to unfair contractual terms. With the enactment of "Council Directive 93/13 EEC of 5 April 1993 on Unfair Terms in Consumer Contracts" a significant step has been made in the process of standardizing this law throughout the European Community. The directive has considerably eased the task of businesses that must remain abreast of the consumer-protection laws in effect in the European countries where they transact business. For the European consumer, the directive provides a reasonable amount of assurance that a minimum standard of consumer protection is granted throughout the Community.

CHAPTER 13

THE FREE MOVEMENT OF GOODS IN THE EC: THE EUROPEAN COURT OF JUSTICE'S "CASSIS" CASE LAW

Alfred Hagen Meyer

I. Introduction

Article 30 of the European Economic Community Treaty (also known as the Treaty of Rome and hereinafter referred to as the EEC Treaty) provides:

> quantitative restrictions on imports and all measures having equivalent effect shall, without prejudice to the following provisions, be prohibited between Member States.

While the European Community (EC) is currently in the process of adopting legislation which implements this provision, the European Court of Justice (ECJ) has already developed a body of case law interpreting Article 30. Many of the court's decisions (in particular its earlier decisions) have strongly encouraged the development of a free market within the EC.

The cases which have subjected national trade restrictions to strict scrutiny and thus represent a very broad interpretation of Article 30's prohibition include: the initial case of "International Fruit Co." (ECJ ECR 1971, 1107), the classic cases "Dassonville" (ECJ ECR 1974, 837) and "Cassis de Dijon" (ECJ ECR 1979, 649 = (1979) 3 CMLR 494), and finally the recent decision "Sauce Hollandaise" (ECJ, EFLR 1996, p. 80). These cases and others which relate to Article 30 of the EEC Treaty are known as "Cassis" Case law. The ECJ established in this case law the principal of "mutual recognition", or. the principle that

> any product from a Community Member State that is legally produced and sold can be marketed in any other Member State.

This all-embracing principal of "mutual recognition" has resulted in the ECJ being flooded with questions by the national courts regarding the compatibility of certain of their nation's regulations with EC law. The mechanism used by the national courts to raise this issue with ECJ is the Preliminary Ruling Procedure. This procedure allows a national court that is handling a case involving a question of EC law to request from the ECJ, in an interlocutory proceeding, a decision on questions of EC law. The national court remains responsible for applying the ECJ's interpretation to the facts of the underlying case and for a final ruling on it.

Apparently being surprised by the number of questions presented and fearing even more, the ECJ felt prompted, in its "Keck" decision, to "reexamine and clarify" [ECJ case C-267 and 268/91, ECR 1993 I, 6097, 6131 (14)] the scope of Article 30.

This chapter will take a look at recent EC case law, trace the debate after "Keck" and attempt to clarify the principles currently governing application of Article 30 of the EEC Treaty.

II. The "Keck" Decision

The "Keck" decision had the effect of raising doubt over whether the ECJ would continue to apply the strong principles encouraging free trade announced in former

"Cassis" case law. To many, it seemed that the "Keck" decision represented a reversal of the court's prior decisions holding that certain cross-border advertising measures violate EC law. This certainly appeared to be the intent of the Court when it said: "contrary to prior jurisdiction . . ." Upon a careful analysis of the ECJ's decision after Keck, however, it can be seen that this decision represented not a complete reversal of prior law but rather a change in direction.

Limiting the scope of Article 30 was probably necessary. In its prior "Oosthoek" decision (ECJ, case 286/81, ECR 1982, 4575), the court had declared that it was a restriction on imports and thus a violation of Article 30 if an enterprise is required

> . . . to either use systems of advertising and sales promotion varying from Member State to Member State or to abandon a system that it believes to be particularly effective.

This decision and the subsequent application of its holding (which came to be known as the "Oosthoek Doctrine") had made the scope of Article 30's application too large. The Oosthoek Doctrine, in conjunction with the Court's holdings that under Article 30 a showing of a potential restraint was sufficient to establish a restriction (ECJ ECR 1975, 181, 198 (14.) - "Sekt") and that a showing of a noticeable impairment of the trade between the Member States was not necessary (ECJ case 16/83, ECR 1984, 1299, 1326 (20.) - "Prantl"), resulted in Article 30 having the potential to prohibit practically all national laws regarding products and marketing.

The ECJ itself justified its decision in "Keck" on grounds of practicality, stating that limiting Article's 30's scope was necessary because participants in business increasingly relied on Article 30 to object to each and every regulation that limits their economic freedom.

III. Sales Terms

In "Keck," the ECJ held that a Member State's law which affects only a foreign supplier's sales terms within the Member State do not constitute a violation of Article 30. The specific regulations concerned in "Keck" impacted only the marketing of imported goods and did not require the foreign supplier to change the product itself or its packaging.

Unfortunately, the ECJ did not define in "Keck" what it meant by "sales terms," and to this day no clear definition exists. Advocate General Attorney Tesauro stated in his final motion in "Hünermund" that "sales terms" are all regulations regarding who is allowed to sell, when, where and how. *Whether* or not one is allowed to sell is not covered in Teasuro's elucidation. The cases since "Keck" have determined that the following regulations constitute sales terms:

- the prohibition of resale below the purchase price (ECJ ECR 1993 I, 6097 - "Keck");
- the pharmacists' professional prohibition concerning the subsidiary line of goods [ECJ ECR 1993, 6787 (21.) - "Hünermund"];
- a prohibition of advertising on television (ECJ EuZW 1995,250-"Leclerc-Siplec");
- the prohibition of pharmacies from selling processed baby milk (ECJ, decision of June 29, 1995, case C-391/92);

- the prohibition of sales that have only a very low profit margin (ECJ, decision of August 11, 1995, case C-63/94);
- regulations providing that the retail trade with tobacco products, irrespective of their origin, is reserved only to admitted distributors (ECJ, decision of December 14, 1995, case C-387/93).

In addition, the prohibition of special events or the prohibition of certain door-to-door sales (ECJ ECR 1989, 1235 - "Buet") are probably prohibitions based on "sales terms." The ECJ has made it clear that regulations on opening hours (ECJ ECR 1994 I, 2355 - "Punto Casa"; ECR 1994 I, 2227- "t'Heuske") are sales terms and this means that legislation which currently governs Sunday trading is not prohibited by Article 30 of the EEC Treaty.

Attempting to determine whether a violation of Article 30 exists on the basis of whether or not a regulation is a "sales term" has been justly criticized as unrealistic. In fact, it is often impossible to differentiate between the individual product and the distribution system chosen to market the product. "Sales terms" can necessitate different advertising concepts or strategies for the product's marketing in the Common Market and thus not only have an effect on the product's appearance but also on its contents.

IV. Restrictions Relating to Goods

The "Keck" decision did maintain that national restrictions relating to the goods themselves, such as, for example, regulations concerning the specification, form, size, weight, contents, appearance, labeling and packaging of a product could constitute a violation of Article 30 (ECJ ECR 1993 I, 6097 -"Keck"). The ECJ reasoned that restrictions which lead to different specifications for one and the same product within the country and in foreign countries undermine a global, uniform marketing strategy in the domestic market and probably result in an increase in the product's costs for packaging, appearance, labeling and advertising. Even if the pertinent national regulations are applied to all products without differentiation, the ECJ considers such national regulations to be an impediment to trade between the Member States.

The ECJ followed this reasoning in its "Mars" decision (ECJ case C-470/93, decision of July 6, 1995), which is discussed below.

V. The "Cassis" Formula

A broad interpretation of the term "measures having equivalent effect" [Art. 30 of the EEC Treaty (see above)] would inevitably lead to tensions between the principles of the free movement of goods and the powers reserved to the Member States. These potentially diverging interests are balanced by application of the "Cassis" formula, which requires an examination of possible legal justifications for the national restriction. Under this balancing formula, national impediments to the free movement of goods resulting from the Member States' differing trade restrictions are examined to determine if the regulation under scrutiny in a given case fulfills an "imperative requirement." First, the ECJ examines the regulation to determine if it relates to important national interests which include but are not limited to the following:

- fiscal control (ECJ ECR 1979, 649, 662 (8.) - "Cassis de Dijon"),
- environmental protection (ECJ ECR 1985, 538, 549 (13. and 15.) - "ADBHU"; case 302/86, ECR 1988,

4607, 4630 (8.) = [1989] 1 CMLR 619 - "Getränkeflaschen"),

- cinematic culture (ECJ ECR 1985, 2605 "Cinéthèque"),
- consumer protection

  - and -
- fair trading.

National regulations on product marketing, advertising and labeling are thus often justified by the need of a Member State to protect the consumer and ensure fair trading within its borders. Second, the regulation at issue must be "imperative," which is to say that it cannot be replaced by another, milder regulation.

This "imperative requirement" criterion is not based on the principle of due course of law but rather on a limitation of national jurisdiction under EC law. According to the principles of EC law, a Member State may pass legislation which has the effect of impairing the creation of the Common Market and limiting the flow of foreign goods into their country only to the extent such legislation is necessary.

VI. The "Mars" Decision

The recent "Mars" decision issued by the ECJ on July 6, 1995 helped to clarify how the "imperative requirement" criterion is applied to a particular set of facts. In that case, the Regional Court of Cologne, Germany, filed a Preliminary Ruling Procedure requesting that the ECJ determine whether a German regulation was compatible with Article 30. The regulation at issue prohibited an ice-cream snack which was produced and legally marketed in France from being marketed in Germany on the grounds that its appearance would likely cause the consumer to expect that the product was offered at the same price as the product with the old appearance, and the design of the words on the label "+ 10 percent ice-cream" could cause the consumer to believe that the product's size or weight has been enlarged or increased to a considerable extent.

In its ruling, the ECJ declared that "the mere possibility that importers and retail traders could raise the price of the product and that on the basis of this fact consumers could be mislead" did not justify requiring the importers to change the product's appearance and label as a precondition to marketing the product in Germany (see ECJ case C-470/93, decision of July 6, 1995, basis for the decision 19 - "Mars").

In order to justify a restriction based on the danger that a product might somehow deceive the customer, the ECJ demands the "ascertainment of clearly and definitely proven events." It is, however, unnecessary to show that a customer has actually been damaged by a deception in the product or its marketing. In its "Nissan" decision, the ECJ stated that the potential deception of a considerable number of consumers is sufficient (ECJ case C-373/90, decision of January 16, 1992; here, see in detail Meyer, wrp 1993, 215.).

Finally, in "Mars" the ECJ interpreted the EC law but, in accordance with the division of responsibility between the two courts in a Preliminary Ruling Procedure, left the application of that law (in this case a factual determination of whether and to what extent deception is present) as well as the final ruling on the underlying case to the national court.

VII. Judicious Consumers

In determining the legal standard to be applied by the national courts under Article 30 for the assessment of a danger of deception, the ECJ takes as a model the consumer who not only has a right to information (ECJ, ECR 1990 I - 667 - "GB-INNO-BM") but who also has a responsibility to acquire information (ECJ, ECR 1990 I - 4828, 4849 - "Pall/Dahlhausen".). In its "Mars" decision, the Court stated

> One can expect from judicious consumers that they know that the size of advertising prints that indicate an increase in the product's amount and the extent of this increase are not necessarily connected.

VIII. Clinique

The Court's reasoning that an assessment of deception should be made based on the "judicious consumer" is not surprising. An examination of prior ECJ case law reveals that the Court has made use of this consumer model for a number of years already. A telling example of this is found in the Court's "Clinique decision " (ECJ case C-315/92, decision of February 2, 1994, „Clinique").

In the early 1970s, the American enterprise Estée Lauder introduced a series of care and decorative cosmetic products as well as various scents under the name "Clinique." These products were produced in Great Britain, Belgium and Switzerland according to identical formulas and marketed in Europe through subsidiaries.

In Germany, the products were marketed in perfumeries and perfumery departments of department stores. In view of Germany's strict regulations contained in section 3 of the Law on Unfair and Misleading Advertising ["Gesetz gegen den unlauteren Wettbewerb" (UWG)], however, the American company chose to use the name "Linique" instead of "Clinique." It was reasoned that the use of the name "Clinique" would trigger in a not insignificant number of consumers a mental association with the fields of health care and medicine. The possibility therefore existed that consumers would attribute a curative effect to the product which it did not have. The use of the product specification "Clinique" was restricted by the publicity provision of section 3 of the Law on Unfair and Misleading Advertising.

In addition, it was assumed that section 27 paragraph 1 of the Food Act ("Lebensmittelgesetz"), which states that "no effects are to be attributed" to cosmetic products "which they do not have according to scientific findings or that are not sufficiently guaranteed by scientific findings" would also be infringed by the use of the name "Clinique."

The ECJ declared that prohibiting the marketing of the cosmetics under the specification "Clinique" was incompatible with Article 6 Paragraph 3 of the Directive on Cosmetics. The ECJ concluded that despite the clinical and/or medical connotation of the product specification "Clinique," the specification does not mislead consumers. With this decision, the ECJ indicated that it proceeds from a model of a consumer who is informed and is able to be informed. The latter point is illustrated by the fact that the ECJ cites its prior decision in the "Pall/Dahlhausen" case. In the "Pall/Dahlhausen" case, the court again indicated that a consumer has the responsibility of acquiring information. The Court observed that cautious participants in business who would like to know whether a trademark is protected in a Member State by an exclusive right can sufficiently inform themselves by using public registers (ECJ case C-

238/89, 13.12.1990, ECR 1990 I 4828, 4849 - "Pall/Dahlhausen".).

IX. Summary

An analysis of ECJ "Cassis" case law (particularly the most recent decisions) indicates that the following principles are important in determining whether a Member State's regulation violates Article 30 of the EEC treaty:

"Keck" formula concerning the applicability of Article 30:

- Does the national regulation effect certain sales terms?
- Examples: sale below original cost, laws on opening hours, Sunday sales

"Dassonville" formula:

- Is the national regulation likely to impair the free movement of goods within the Community directly or indirectly, actually or potentially?
- Examples: trade details referring to the product's specification, form, size, weight, contents, appearance, labeling and packaging

"Cassis de Dijon" formula:

- Is the regulation necessary due to "imperative requirements"; for example, does the regulation protect the consumer or ensure fair trade and is it in proportion to the harm which it addresses?

"Imperative requirement":

- Does the regulation serve an "imperative requirement" by virtue of its justification under Article 36 of the EEC Treaty which reserves to the Member States the power to provide for public order?

Chapter 14

TRADEMARK PROTECTION IN EUROPE

Paul W. McGuire

I. Recent Developments

Two new international trademark conventions which promise several advantages for non-European applicants came into force in 1996. The Community Trademark Convention provides for protection throughout the European Union on the basis of a single application. The new Madrid Protocol represents an amendment of the Madrid Agreement, which should make filing more attractive to applicants from the United States, Japan, Canada and Australia.

A. The Community Trademark Convention

1. Coverage and advantages

The new Community Trademark Convention covers the Member States of the European Union, which currently includes the following fifteen countries, with a total population of about 360 million.

EU Countries

Austria	Germany	Netherlands
Belgium	Greece	Portugal
Denmark	Ireland	Spain
Finland	Italy	Sweden
France	Luxembourg	United Kingdom

Prior to the introduction of the Community Trademark, if a non-European company wanted to register its trademark in Europe and if the company had no subsidiary (place of business) in Europe, it was necessary to file an individual application in each country. Of the aforementioned fifteen EU states, this sometimes meant correspondence with fifteen different attorneys and applications filed in eleven different official languages. It's not hard to imagine the costs and the confusion which existed. Normally, just a few relevant countries were picked for filing.

The Trademark Convention not only provides the possibility of a single application for all EU countries; a directive of the EU also requires that the Member States harmonize their trademark laws. This has been done in the meantime. Nevertheless, differences remain concerning enforcement of trademarks against competitors, counterfeiters and pirates.

The European Union basically includes that which is commonly understood as Western Europe. In the future, Eastern Europe will become increasingly important, however, it is difficult to predict how its trademark law will develop. Central and Eastern Europe comprise almost thirty territories or newly formed states which have emerged from what was formerly the "Soviet Block." The opening of borders for trade has given rise to a new wave of counterfeiting and piracy. These territories or states have, in the meantime, established patent and trademark laws; however, implementation is very slow. Even though trademarks and patents can be protected, the procedures and courts for enforcing rights is very limited. Despite this unhappy situation, it is sometimes advisable to obtain patents or trademarks which can be used as bargaining chips in joint venture negotiations.

2. Filing and costs of a CMT application

The Trademark Office is located in Alicante, Spain and is officially known as the Office for Harmonization in the Internal Trademarket (OHIM). Alicante, itself, is located on the Mediterranean coast of Spain and has a reputation as an attractive holiday resort area.

To file a trademark, non-Europeans such as Americans or Canadians must be represented by an attorney who practices in one of the member countries. A CTM application need not be based on an earlier national application, although filing will often be based on a priority claim. The CTM can be filed in any of the official languages of the EU: English, French, German, Italian or Spanish. In addition, the applicant must specify one alternative language which could be used, for example, in the case of possible opposition proceedings. The filing in Alicante can be made by electronic mail or facsimile.

The Trademark Convention provides for the payment of official fees based on the ECU currency. The filing fee is about $1,300; and, assuming no objections are made by OHIM, the registration fee is about $1,400. About $1,000 may be added for attorney expenses in a typical application. While the total filing costs are not small, they are certainly a bargain compared to the costs of filing in 15 different countries.

3. Examination and registration

Upon application, the Trademark Office will perform a search of prior trademarks to determine whether an identical or similar trademark has been filed for the same class of goods. The results of this search are not used as grounds for refusing the application but are sent to the owners of relevant trademarks found in the search. These persons may then later oppose registration of the trademark.

The application can be rejected by the Trademark Office on the basis of absolute grounds; for instance, lack of inherent distinctiveness. Relative grounds, such as conflicts with existing identical trademarks mentioned above, are only be handled in opposition proceedings. On a more curious note, the registration of profane or derogatory words is understandably prohibited. In the Community Trademark system, however, eleven different languages are to be considered and a perfectly acceptable word in one language may be highly obscene in another language. Such cases have already arisen, for example, with the proposed word "Puta."

4. Opposition

An opposition period of three months runs from the publication date of the application, within which the owner of any conflicting trademark may file opposition. The opposition proceedings are held before the OHIM in Alicante. If refused, the application can still be converted into separate national applications in the countries where no conflicting prior rights exist. Decisions from the OHIM can first be appealed to the Board of Appeal and if necessary, a subsequent appeal can be made to the European Court of Justice.

The Community Trademark is valid for a period of ten years, after which renewal is possible without proof of use. Validity of the trademark, however, does require some use. Under the Community Trademark Convention, use in any part of the European Union is sufficient. For example, even if the trademark is only used in the UK, protection is maintained in all fifteen EU countries. A Community Trademark may be subject to cancellation upon application to OHIM if it is not used for over a period of five years in any part of the Union.

5. Seniority

In many cases, a company will already have national registrations of their trademarks in various European countries. The so-called "seniority claim" allows such companies to transfer their national rights into one Community Trademark which can be extended to cover all fifteen EU states.

6. Litigation and licenses

Infringement actions with respect to the Community Trademark are dealt with by the respective national courts in the member countries. This may be one disadvantage of the system since even despite the recent harmonization of the national trademark laws, some differences in interpretation still exist.

An infringement action is usually filed in the country where the infringement occurred. Specific courts which have jurisdiction to hear such cases have been designated in each Member State. The Convention Trademark Convention has provided that an injunction obtained against an infringer from one of these courts is effective throughout the entire EU. By so doing, the Convention has greatly simplified the policing of trademark infringers anywhere within the EU. Previously, one had to enforce a trademark separately in each country.

Assignments or licenses of the Community Trademark are registered at the Trademark Office (OHIM). Being unitary, the trademark cannot be assigned separately to different parties for different countries. One can however assign licenses to different parties for different territories.

B. Procedures at the border

A new 1995 regulation of the European Community provides means for confiscating imported goods which infringe a Community Trademark. Under the regulation, a system is established by which the customs authorities can now seize and in some cases destroy goods which infringe trademarks, copyrights and even designs. The provisions extend to all customs operations including, among others, import, export, re-export and transit operations.

If the owners of a trademark suspects that infringing goods will be imported, they can file an application with the designated national authority and the authority's customs officials will seize the goods. If the infringer opposes the seizure, the trademark holder is allowed a period of twenty working days to prove that legal action has been initiated against the infringer.

The new EU regulation also provides the possibility of the customs officials intervening on their own when suspicious or obviously pirated goods are imported. In this case, the suspected goods can be held for up to three working days. The trademark owner is informed of the good's detention and is invited to file an application for seizure and destruction. Experience up until now has been that the degree of interest shown by the customs officials to watch out for suspicious goods varies greatly from country to country. The general trend, however, is to treat violations of the trademark laws at the border more seriously than in the past.

C. The Madrid Protocol

1. Parties to the Protocol

The Madrid Protocol, like the existing Madrid Agreement, will be administered by the World Intellectual Property Organization (W.I.P.O.) in Geneva. It is expected that all countries of the European Union will join the Madrid Protocol as well as other countries which are not currently party to the Madrid Agreement. Moreover, it is hoped that non-European countries such as the United States, Canada, Australia and Japan would eventually ratify the Protocol.

Another advantage would be that the OHIM is expected to become a member of the Protocol. And if this occurs, an application under the Madrid Protocol would allow the designation of the EU for regional protection. Conversely, a CTM application could serve as a priority claim when filing an international application under the Protocol.

2. Application procedures

Application is still restricted to nationals or legal entities of a member state of the Protocol. In addition, the application must be based on a national application in a home country. In contrast to the CTM, where coverage is provided in all fifteen EU countries, applicants can select the particular countries where they want the trademark to be valid.

Although the Madrid Protocol provides for a unified application, the respective national trademark offices of the designated countries will separately examine the application under their own national provisions. The examination procedure and the criteria for examination will then vary from country to country. For example, the UK examines an application on both absolute and relative grounds, while a country such as Germany does not examine an application for conflicts with existing registrations. In addition, if objections from any respective national office arise, it will be necessary for the applicant to appoint a local representative to handle matters before that national office.

Following registration under the Protocol, the applicant acquires a bundle of national rights, and use of the trademark must be proven in each of the countries designated in order to maintain validity of the trademark in that country. This latter requirement represents a disadvantage compared to the Community Trademark system. It may be easier, however, to register trademarks in at least some countries using the Madrid Protocol rather than the Community Trademark system. In addition, one is not putting all of one's eggs in one basket as with the Community Trademark system.

3. Assignment and litigation

A registration under the Madrid Protocol does not result in the granting of a unitary right as it does under the CTM. Thus, it will be possible to assign the trademark right on a country by country basis. The registration will have a duration of ten years; it can be renewed centrally at the W.I.P.O. office, and no proof of use is required upon renewal.

Infringement and validity suits with respect to the international trademark will be handled by the national courts under their respective national provisions. Unlike the CTM, a judgment obtained in one country is only enforceable in that country. To attack an international trademark under the Madrid Protocol, it will have to be attacked separately in each of the countries covered.

II. Abuses of the Trademark System

As in many non-European countries, the European trademark system can and is abused by "trademark sharks." Such persons anticipate the new trademarks a company intends to use and files for corresponding protection. For example, it is not uncommon for Europeans traveling in the U.S. to pick up new names for new successful products and then go back to Europe and file for the trademark. When the U.S. company gets around to trademarketing in Europe, they find the trademark already registered and are often forced to pay considerable sums to acquire their "own" trademark. Amounts of up to $50,000 are not uncommon depending on the product and its commercial value.

A particularly extreme case of such abuse involves the new series of medium-sized cars of Mercedes-Benz called the "E-Klasse." Mercedes had filed an application at the German Patent Office, however, the trademark was rejected on the grounds that it was descriptive. On the other hand, a certain Mr. Scheele obtained registration for the trademark “Classe-E” in Switzerland, France and Germany. Apparently Mr. Scheele had better luck at the German Patent Office.

Mr. Scheele approached Mercedes-Benz in order to “settle” the problem of collision as he understood it. According to press reports, Mercedes paid about $140,000 to buy the rights for Switzerland and France. For Germany, Mr. Scheele demanded a license fee of about $700 for each car of the E-Klasse. Assuming that Mercedes sells at least 100 cars per day of this series, he was demanding $70,000 per day.

Mercedes-Benz has taken legal action before the District Court of Frankfurt and requested a declaratory judgment that Mr. Scheele has no claims to the German trademark. It is argued that he acted in bad faith when filing for the trademark, his only intention being to subsequently obtain license royalties. Mr. Scheele, on the other hand, purports to be a trademark “inventor,” a creative profession which he undertakes independently of any particular manufacturer or any particular product. He apparently feels it proper that he should be rewarded when his creative instincts are successful.

A promising argument of Mercedes-Benz would appear to be prior use of the trademark. Although the “E-Klasse” series was not yet sold on the trademarket, Mercedes had undertaken advertising in car magazines and demonstration cars were available. A decision of the District Court is still outstanding and however the case is decided, an appeal can be expected.

One lesson to be learned is that persistence before the trademark offices pays off, especially on the matter of distinctiveness. For important trademarks, a parallel Community Trademark application would be advisable.

For non-Europeans, it should also be kept in mind that abuse also occurs in Europe and not just at home. Early filings in Europe can avoid considerable conflict and costs at a later date.